78-02569

694   Jaber, William
J   Tree houses; how to build your own tree house.   Drake
     ©1975

1 Carpentry   I Title

694

METRO Catalog Cards

Tree Houses

TREE HOUSES

How to Build Your Own Tree House

by William Jaber

Drake Publishers, Inc.

New York   **London**

694   78-02569

Published in 1975 by

Drake Publishers, Inc.

381 Park Avenue South

New York, New York 10016

Library of Congress Cataloging in Publication Data

Jaber, William

    TREE HOUSES

ISBN: 0-8473-1021-3

LC: 75-109-43

Printed in the United States of America

To the memory of Thomas Maynard (1899–1967)
His wisdom came not from schools but from living in
harmony with God and his West Virginia mountains

BOY IN A TREE

No safer refuge than a tree
  to keep small boy from deviltry —

His haven, friend and battleground
his lookout tower, his high-walled town
his meeting place, his secret spot
for dreaming of his future loy

If he climbs well, he can be
astronaut in Gemini
or — topmost branch his launching tower —
titan missiles blast to power.

If his, by chance, an apple tree
he can pellet endlessly.
If — in the fall — a gingko old
he can cull a pot of gols

High above the hemlock's breeze
he can watch the chickadees.
When it is raining, he will be
soaked in sweet security.

Mothers ! Never worry, please,
if your small boy takes to trees

By Katherine Earls Gerwin, 1973

From the pages of St. Anthony Messenger
Volume 83, Number 3, August 1975

TABLE OF CONTENTS

TREE HOUSES

How to Build Your Own Tree House

INTRODUCTION

Tree houses are fun. They are fun to build and fun to spend time in. A tree house is easy to build. And when it is finished it becomes many things to the builder --- limited only by the imagination. A tree house could be the bridge room of an ocean liner or the control cabin of a big transcontinental airliner. A tree house could be a castle, or it could be the main room of the command module in a space ship, outward bound on a long voyage of exploration.

But to everyone , at sometime, a tree house can be a refuge --- a place where one can be alone, and think his own private thoughts. It is a hideaway where friends can meet in secret, or where a private anger can be worked off.

Anyone who has ever built a tree house knows the feelings of joy and pride that comes from making something real and useful with one's own hands. Building a tree house has so many rewards that it is worth the best efforts of a single builder or the cooperative action of a group.

At first thought, a tree house might seem to be hard to build. It might also seem -- to a parent, especially -- to be a little dangerous. But such thoughts are valid only if the project is attempted without any guide or plan, and without the proper tools to work with, and some basic knowledge about how to handle tools and materials safely. In addition to these considerations, we caution that the tree is a living thing and can be injured or even killed if any structure is built in to it without guidance and knowledge.

The author has made a strong effort to help supply the plan and sequence of procedures to be followed, so that the builder can be informed, carefull, and safe in the work. It is also hoped that the book will prove a valuable guide in the use of materials, tools and for the adoption of safe rules for any kind of carpentry or woodwork. The shadow s of expert carpenters and con-struction engineers linger in the background of this book. Their advice and comments have become a part of the work and preparation of the book.

Although expert advice has been followed to produce the clearest possible instructions, no prior knowledge of carpentry or of the building trades is assumed for the tree house builder. This book is for those of us who must work, for the most part, with used materials and scrap lumber -- anything that will suit our purpose and which we can find laying around in out back-yards and cellars.

The lumberyard people have a special grade of lumber which they call "common" or "second" grade lumber. It is usually cheaper to buy. This type of lumber has knots, knotholes and other defects, but nothing about this lumber would prevent it from being used in the tree house.

This book is presented as a guide to all the urgent major considerations in building a tree house. It offers a suggested sequence of procedures, and it passes on to the reader many tips on how to use tools, how to work safely, and how to avoid injury to the tree.

TREES FOR TREE HOUSES ?

What makes a good site for a tree house

The arrangement of a tree's trunk, or trunks, and the pattern of its branches
with respect to the ground, are the main elements that determine if the tree
will make a good site for a tree house.   Most pine trees are not suitable. But
a few of the other evergreens, such as the live oak, do often provide good
sites. It is the deciduous group of trees – those that shed their leaves seasonally --
that form most of the good sites for tree houses.

In order to be a site for a tree house , there must be at least three points
at the same level in the tree where the corners of a tree house platform could
be attached.   For example, the old sycamore, shown on the next page,
has the minimum number of points, formed by the arrangement and angle
of its three trunks.

But most good sites will have four points at the same level. The best
sites are those provided by trees whose trunks divide into two major limbs
at about 8 feet off the ground, and which also contain one or two large
branches at lower levels in the tree.

The northern catalpa tree, shown here, is hardy, and grows nearly everywhere
in the United States.   The long seedpods remain after the leaves fall, making
the tree easy to recognize in winter. As the drawing shows, this tree provides a
good solid four-point level for a foundation platform that is roughly rectangular
in shape.   There is enough space overhead free of branches to make possible
adding walls and a low roof to this house.

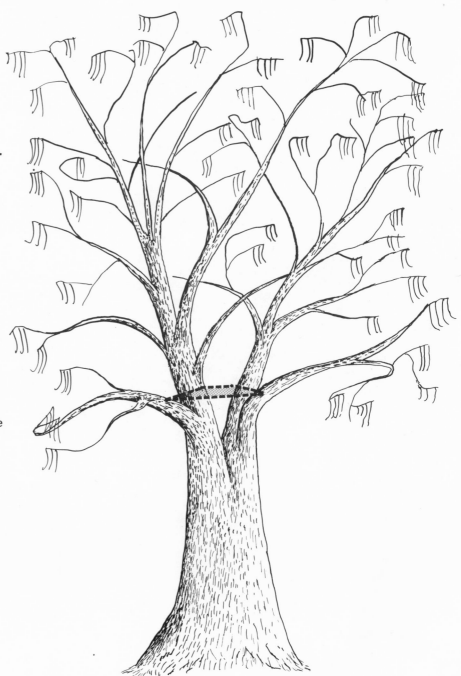

1

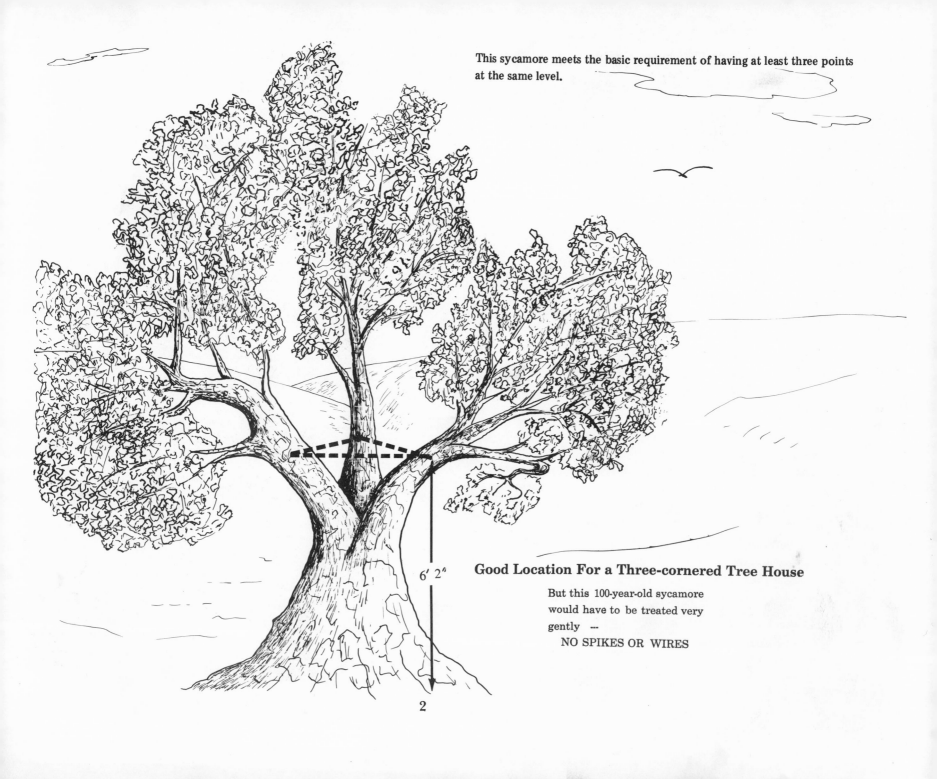

This sycamore meets the basic requirement of having at least three points at the same level.

6' 2"

Good Location For a Three-cornered Tree House

But this 100-year-old sycamore would have to be treated very gently ---

NO SPIKES OR WIRES

2

Silver maple

Some kinds of trees of North America that very often make good sites for tree houses

Black oak

Southern hackberry

White ash

Baobab

River red gum

Snow gum eucalyptus

Bottle tree

SOME TREES OUTSIDE NORTH AMERICA THAT OFTEN MAKE GOOD SITES FOR TREE HOUSES

MATERIALS

Although the plan of construction outlined in this book is based on the use of scrap lumber and cast-off materials, the builder should exercise caution in using old materials without having the special knowledge that experts have in their use. For example, asbestos that has been thrown away has many hazards to health, and the dangers in using old plate glass should be obvious.

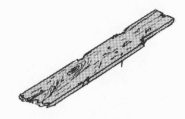

All the materials should be clean and free of sharp edges, rusty nails, metal projections, glass, and splinters. Plywood, chipboard, gypsumboard, cardboard, tarpaper, canvas, linoleum, and fruit boxing are examples of materials that can be used.

The lumberyard sells a common or second grade of lumber that is much less expensive to buy. It has knots, knotholes, and other defects, but it is suitable for use in the tree house. When ordering, disregard the terms "soft," and "hard." They are usually meaningless to amateur builders. If you stick to pine, hemlock, cedar and poplar, you will have wood that can be cut and nailed easily.

Decay of wood occurs only in the presence of water -- there is no such thing as "dry rot" in wood. To protect your wood from decay, waterproof all the surfaces by painting or by soaking the pieces in creosote. But do not use any preservatives or household paints on the tree itself.

Use nothing larger than 2" x 4" lumber. Even the frame of the platform can be made of 2" x 4" lumber. This can be purchased in measured lengths from the lumber yard. The low-grade seconds are adequate, and cost much less than first grade lumber. Unless you are buying rough lumber, when you ask for 2" x 4", the actual dimensions of the lumber will be slightly less, due to the finishing process.

Walls and siding can be made from chipboard, clapboard, fiberboard, plywood, or even a good reinforced cardboard, tacked over a good framework. See the pages on the construction of the wall .

Roofing should be of tarpaper, or some light material, tacked over the fafters, fashioned from 2" x 4" lumber. See the pages on making the roof.

You will need rope for ladders, and for lashing and suspending.

6

TOOLS and THEIR USE

All tools should be kept clean and dry to prevent rusting. Never leave them in the tree or lying around where small children can get a hold of them. If the work is halted for more than a day, gather up all the tools and put them back in their usual places. There is nothing more frustrating than looking for a favorite hammer or saw and being unable to find it.

There is a right way and a wrong way to use tools.   If you are not sure about how to use a particular tool, get help.   Some tools, such as saws and planes can be damaged beyond repair by improper use, and others, such as axes and hatchets, can be dangerous.

Do not use razor blades for cutting on wood.

Read carefully the pages on materials, tools and safety. The author cautions the builder not to attempt the project without proper tools or materials, and wihtout regard for the life of the tree and the safety of others.

SAWING   1
Some popular saws

Ripsaw

Used to cut along with the grain of the wood

Coping saw

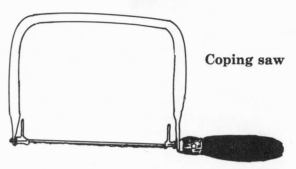

Designed for cutting curves and irregular shapes in the wood. Its teeth are similar to those of a crosscut saw.

Crosscut saw

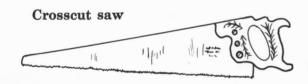

Used to cut across the grain of the wood.

Back saw or miter box saw

Used for making fine cuts. Its teeth are similar to those of a crosscut saw.

Used for cutting metal.

Hacksaw

Keyhole saw

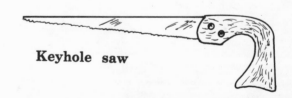

Similar to the coping saw in its use. Its teeth are like those of the ripsaw.

Helpful hints for sawing

Use the proper kind of saw for a particular job. Most saws are classifed as either ripsaws or crosscut saws. Like people, they can be identified by their teeth. The two main types of teeth used for common handsaws are shown here. The size of any saw is determined by the length of the blade in inches. Handsaws come in in sizes 14 to 30 inches.

> Never cut metal with a saw that is designed to cut only wood.

CROSSCUT SAW

Each tooth is a two-edged knife which can cut in either direction. In the back stroke it scores — makes a preliminary cut, so that in the main forward stroke the crosscut saw will cut deeply without splintering the wood. Because of this it is best for cutting across the grain of the wood.

RIP SAW

Each tooth is a tiny chisel. Its cutting action is only in one direction. Each of the chisels cut out a piece of wood on the forward stroke. This is best for cutting with the grain.

> **WHEN A SAW BINDS OR STICKS**
>
> Do not force the blade. If the saw binds it indicates that one of three things is wrong: 1) the wood is too green; 2) the blade is rusted or is covered with some substance such as resin or oil; 3) the blade has too little "set"—the distance the teeth project to the sides. In the latter case, the blade has to be sharpened, and then reset.

The crosscut saw usually has 7 teeth per inch.

The ripsaw usually has 4½ teeth per inch.

HAMMERS and HAMMERING

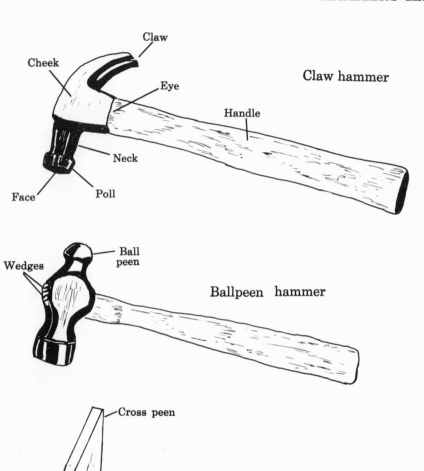

Claw hammer

Claw

Cheek

Eye

Handle

Neck

Face   Poll

Ball peen

Wedges

Ballpeen hammer

Cross peen

Riveting hammer

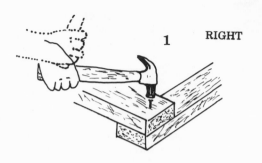

1   RIGHT

WRONG

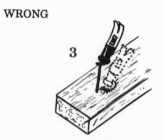

2

3

Hammering

When using a hammer, grasp the handle near the end, and make sure the handle is horizontal to the board when it hits the nail. See Figure 1 above.

Figure 3 shows what happens when you hammer the wrong way, as in Fig. 2

Other Handy Tools you may need While Building the Tree House

Carpenter's rule

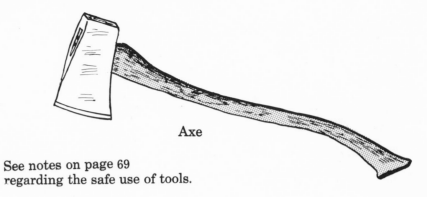

Axe

See notes on page 69 regarding the safe use of tools.

Wood chisel

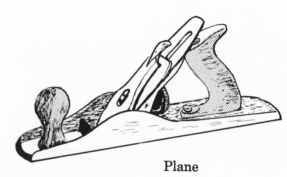

Plane

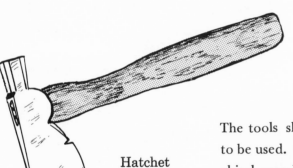

Hatchet

The tools shown in these pages are those most likely to be used. Other tools, such as pliers, or a wood chisel, may be useful occasionally. Extreme care should be taken when using tools up in a tree, because if you drop any tools, someone under the tree could be seriously injured.

Screwdriver

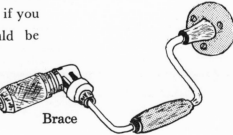

Brace

NAILS

Nails are better than screws for tree houses since nails will be less rigid, allowing for some tree motion.

Common nails

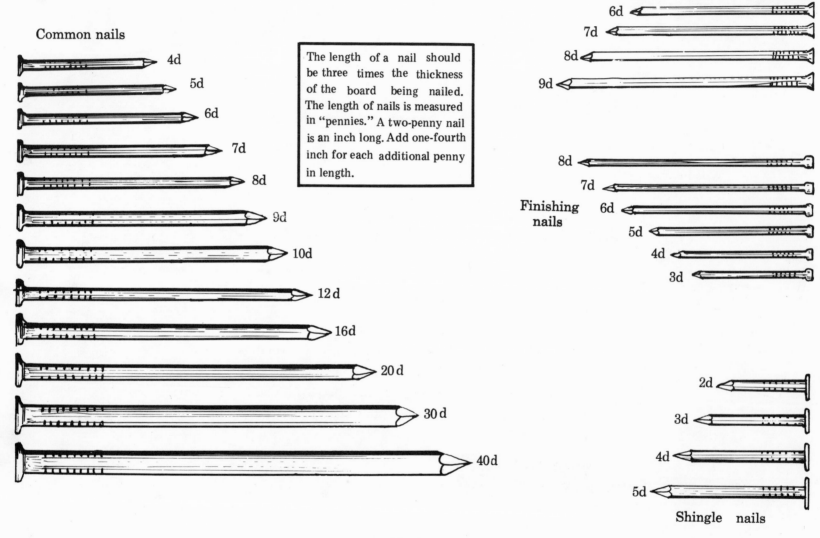

The length of a nail should be three times the thickness of the board being nailed. The length of nails is measured in "pennies." A two-penny nail is an inch long. Add one-fourth inch for each additional penny in length.

Common nails:
4d
5d
6d
7d
8d
9d
10d
12d
16d
20d
30d
40d

Casing nails:
3d
4d
5d
6d
7d
8d
9d

Finishing nails:
8d
7d
6d
5d
4d
3d

Shingle nails:
2d
3d
4d
5d

HOW BIG WILL IT BE?

The size of your tree house will depend on the distance between the limbs or trunks to be spanned by the flooring platform.   The house in this picture is necessarily small because the trunks and branches of this franklin tree are close together.   The house occupies only the free space above the platform.   It is low-set, and is reached by a ladder.

No dimensions will be given because sizes and lengths will vary with the shape and position of branches.

THE FRAME OF THE PLATFORM POSITIONED IN THE TREE

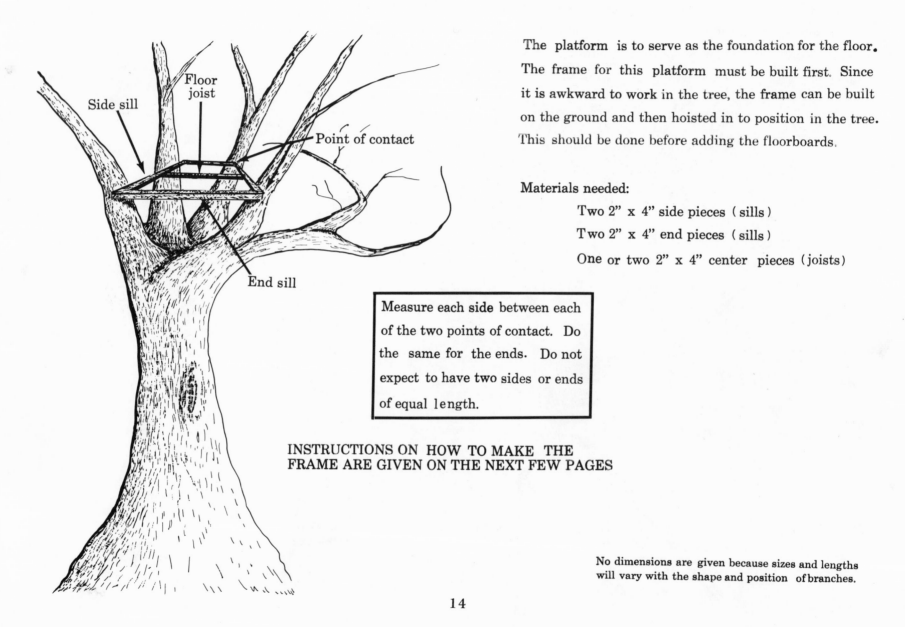

Side sill

Floor joist

Point of contact

End sill

The platform is to serve as the foundation for the floor. The frame for this platform must be built first. Since it is awkward to work in the tree, the frame can be built on the ground and then hoisted in to position in the tree. This should be done before adding the floorboards.

Materials needed:

    Two 2" x 4" side pieces (sills)

    Two 2" x 4" end pieces (sills)

    One or two 2" x 4" center pieces (joists)

> Measure each side between each of the two points of contact. Do the same for the ends. Do not expect to have two sides or ends of equal length.

INSTRUCTIONS ON HOW TO MAKE THE FRAME ARE GIVEN ON THE NEXT FEW PAGES

No dimensions are given because sizes and lengths will vary with the shape and position of branches.

MAKING THE PLATFORM FRAME CORNERS BY JOINING END SILLS WITH SIDE SILLS

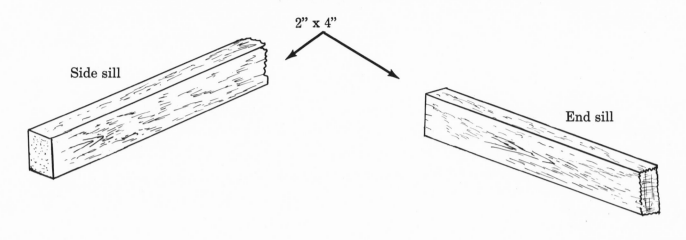

2" x 4"

Side sill

End sill

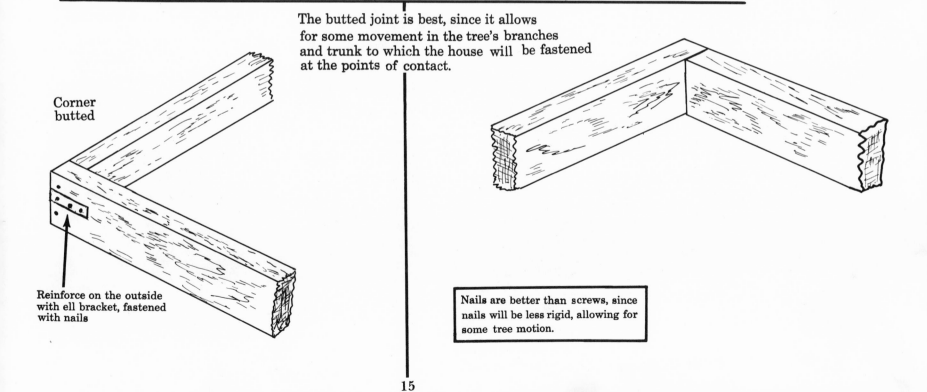

The butted joint is best, since it allows
for some movement in the tree's branches
and trunk to which the house will be fastened
at the points of contact.

Corner
butted

Reinforce on the outside
with ell bracket, fastened
with nails

Nails are better than screws, since
nails will be less rigid, allowing for
some tree motion.

MAKING THE FRAME and
ADDING FLOOR JOISTS

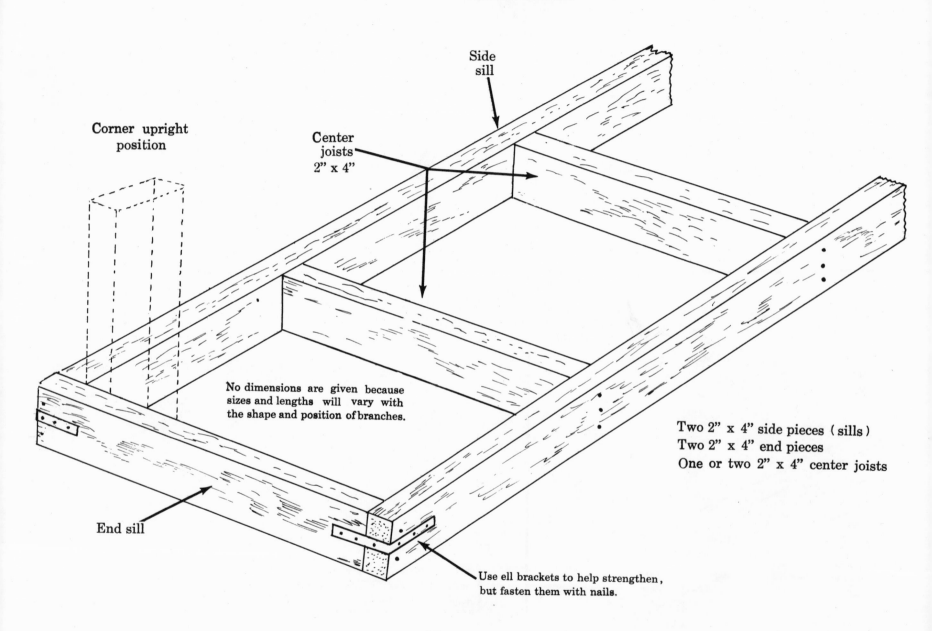

Side
sill

Corner upright
position

Center
joists
2" x 4"

No dimensions are given because
sizes and lengths will vary with
the shape and position of branches.

Two 2" x 4" side pieces (sills)
Two 2" x 4" end pieces
One or two 2" x 4" center joists

End sill

Use ell brackets to help strengthen,
but fasten them with nails.

HOW TO ANCHOR THE PLATFORM FRAME TO THE TREE AT THE POINTS OF CONTACT

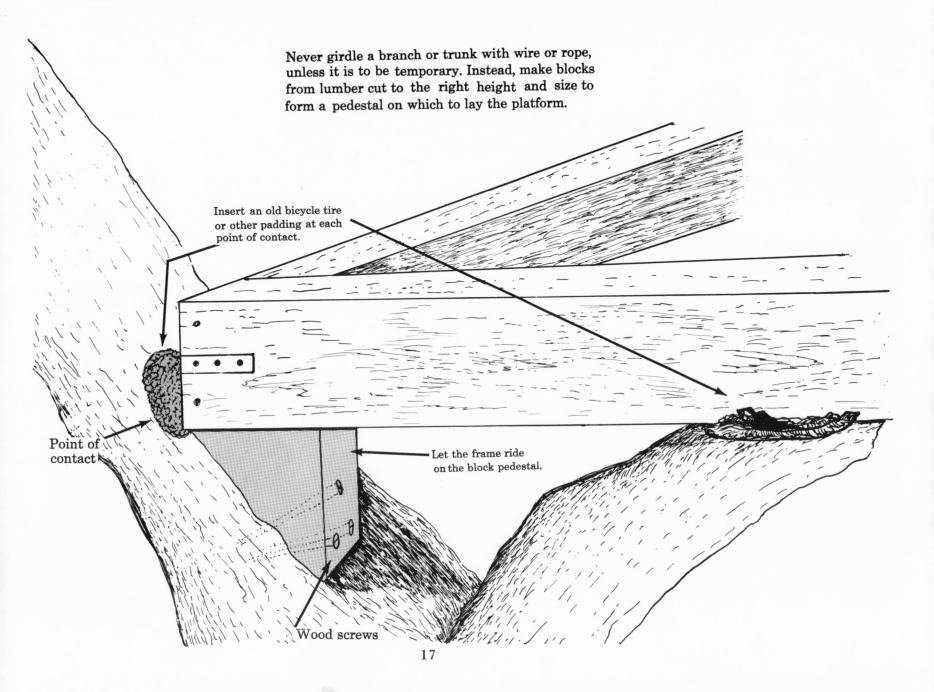

Never girdle a branch or trunk with wire or rope, unless it is to be temporary. Instead, make blocks from lumber cut to the right height and size to form a pedestal on which to lay the platform.

Insert an old bicycle tire or other padding at each point of contact.

Point of contact

Let the frame ride on the block pedestal.

Wood screws

CORNER UPRIGHTS

Nails are better than screws, since nails
will be less rigid, allowing for some tree
motion.

Corner uprights butted in place

Corner
upright

Side sill

End sill

Use ell brackets to help strengthen ,
but fasten them with nails.

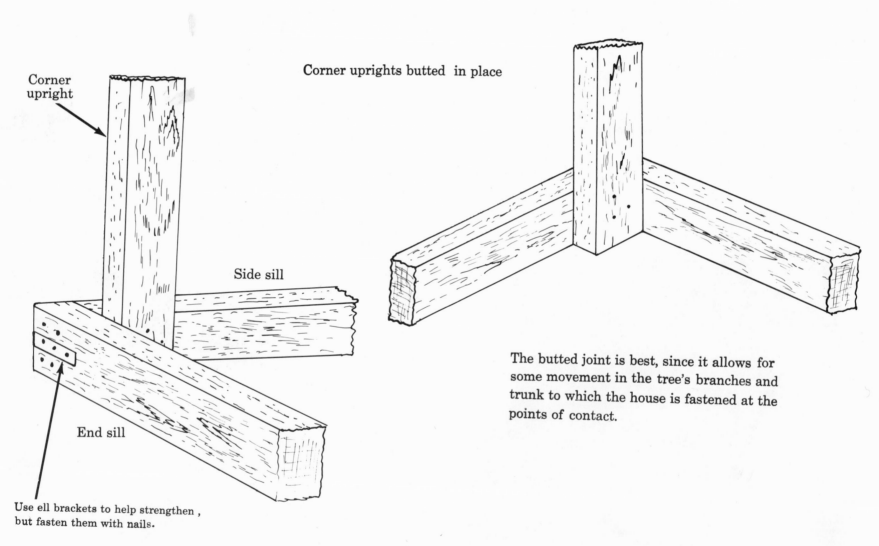

The butted joint is best, since it allows for
some movement in the tree's branches and
trunk to which the house is fastened at the
points of contact.

18

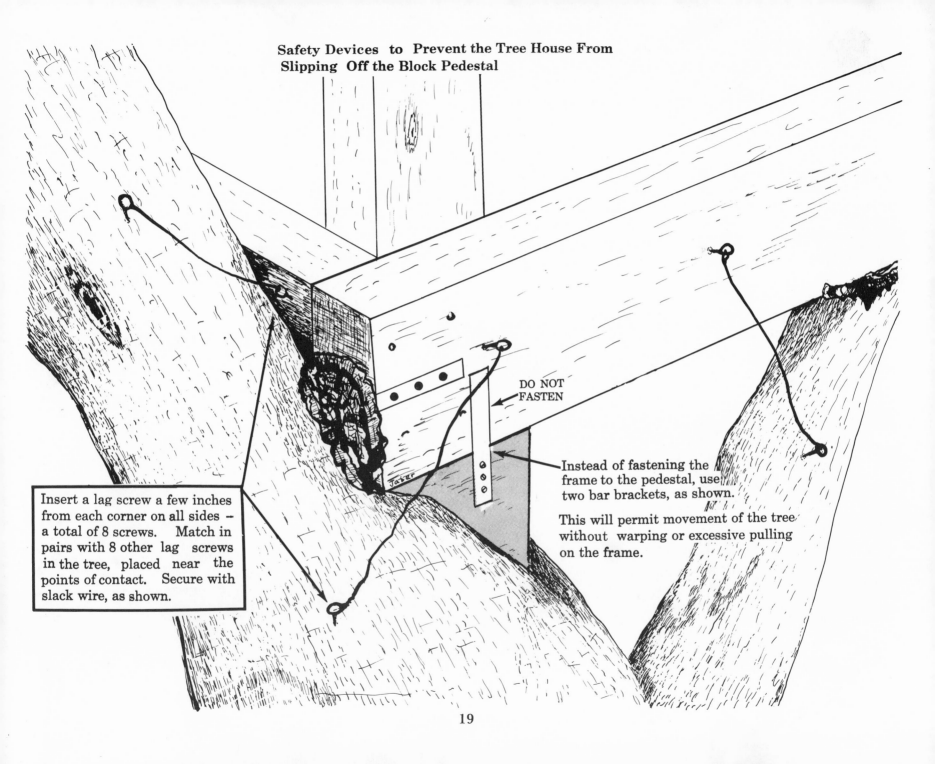

Safety Devices to Prevent the Tree House From Slipping Off the Block Pedestal

DO NOT
FASTEN

Insert a lag screw a few inches from each corner on all sides -- a total of 8 screws.   Match in pairs with 8 other lag screws in the tree, placed near the points of contact.   Secure with slack wire, as shown.

Instead of fastening the frame to the pedestal, use two bar brackets, as shown.

This will permit movement of the tree without warping or excessive pulling on the frame.

19

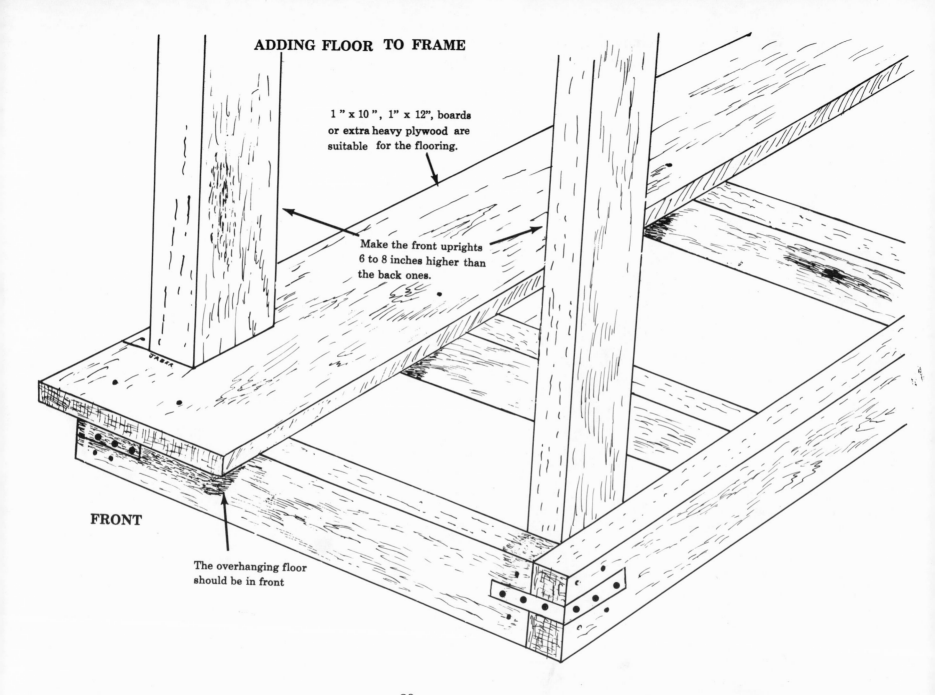

ADDING FLOOR TO FRAME

1 " x 10 ", 1" x 12", boards or extra heavy plywood are suitable for the flooring.

Make the front uprights 6 to 8 inches higher than the back ones.

FRONT

The overhanging floor should be in front

20

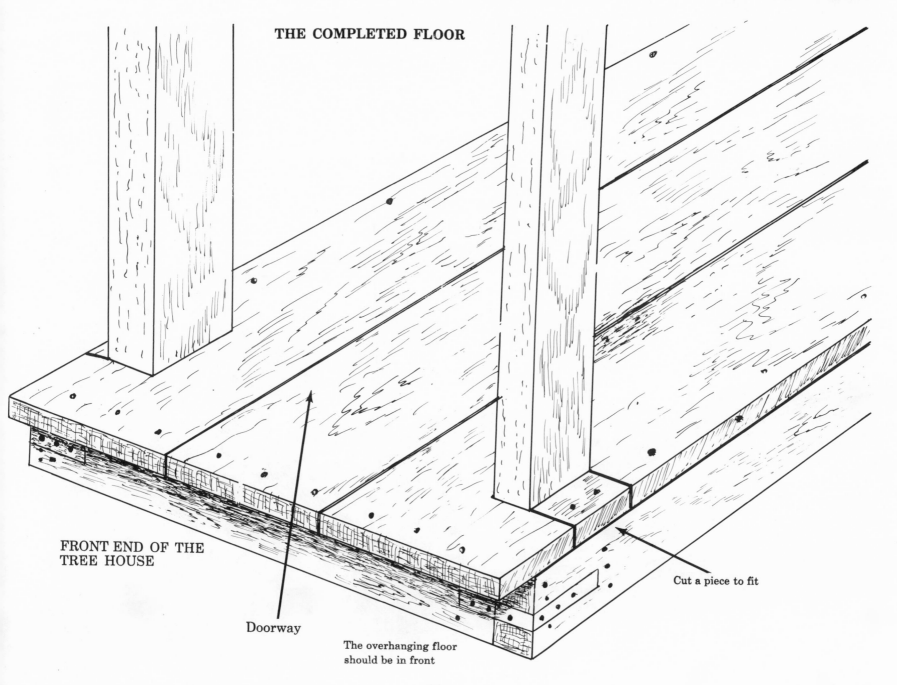

THE COMPLETED FLOOR

FRONT END OF THE
TREE HOUSE

Doorway

The overhanging floor
should be in front

Cut a piece to fit

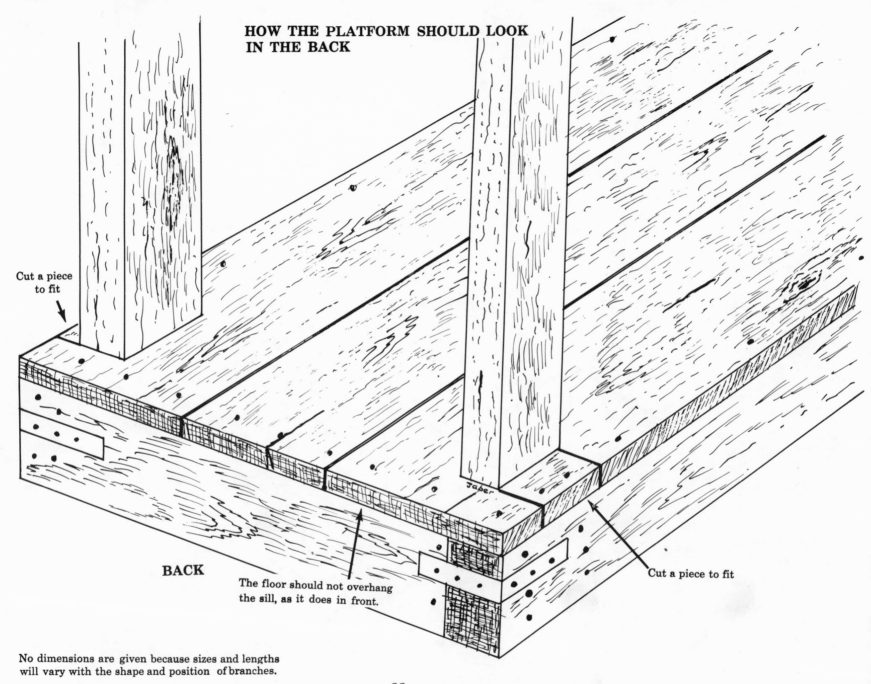

HOW THE PLATFORM SHOULD LOOK IN THE BACK

Cut a piece to fit

Cut a piece to fit

BACK

The floor should not overhang the sill, as it does in front.

No dimensions are given because sizes and lengths will vary with the shape and position of branches.

22

ADDING SIDE AND BACK TOP WALL PLATES

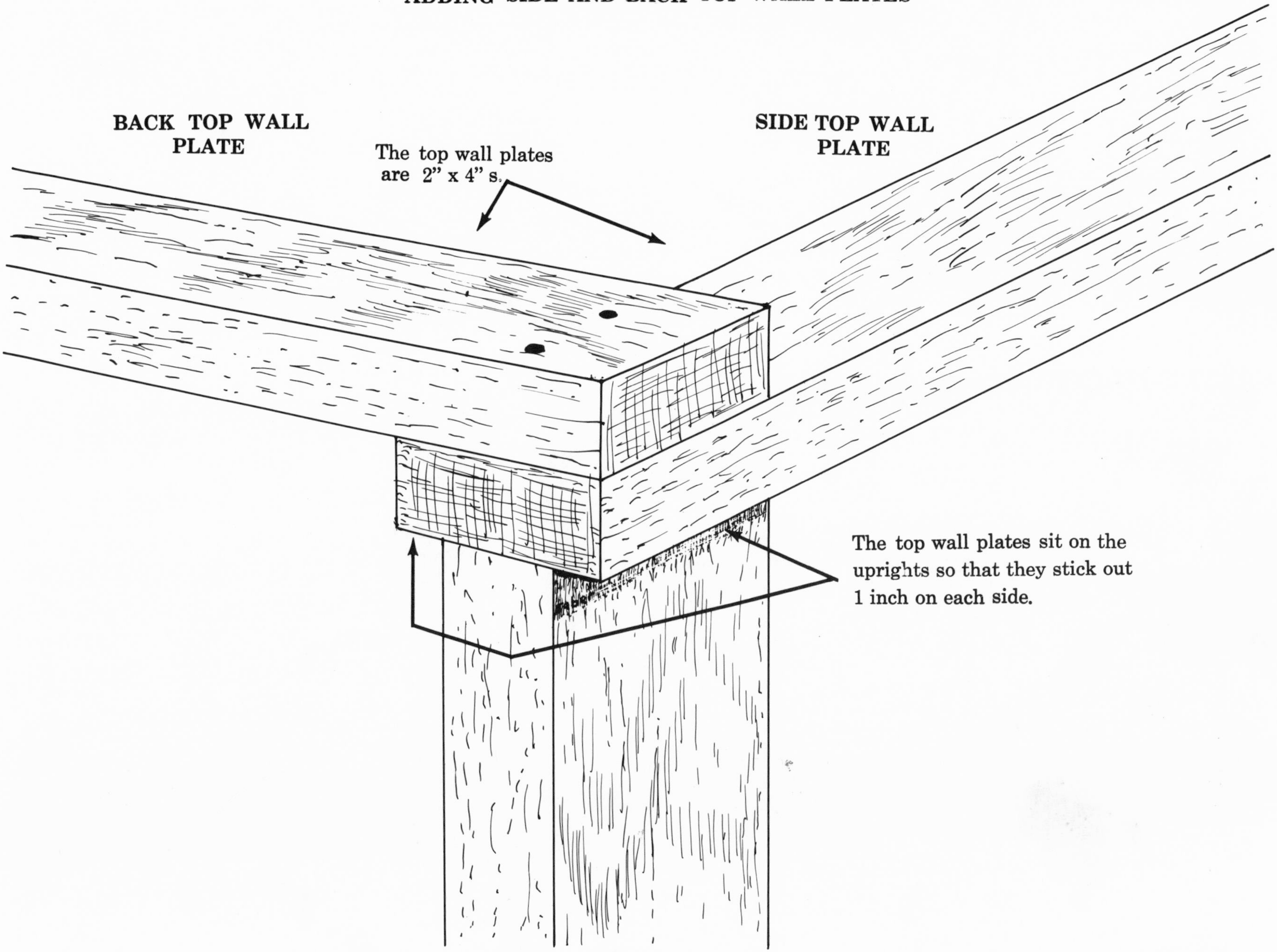

BACK TOP WALL PLATE

SIDE TOP WALL PLATE

The top wall plates are 2" x 4"s.

The top wall plates sit on the uprights so that they stick out 1 inch on each side.

23

ADDING THE DOOR LINTEL

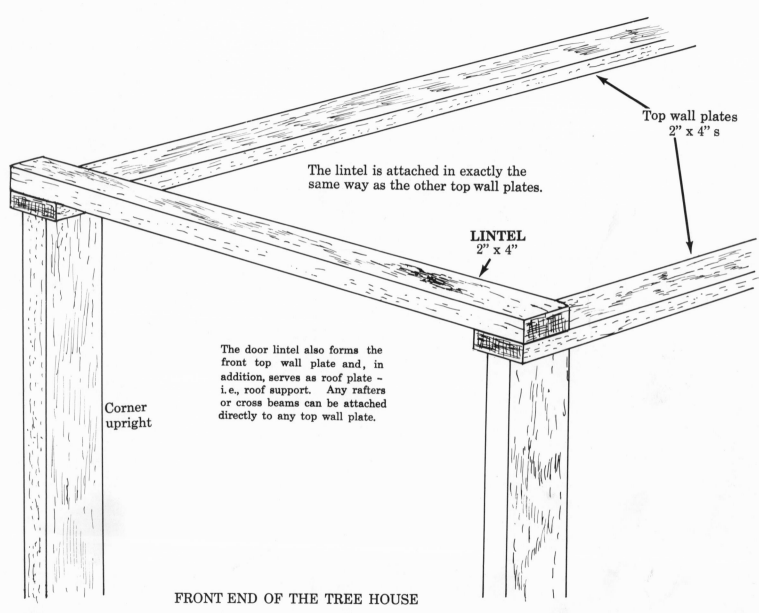

Top wall plates
2" x 4" s

The lintel is attached in exactly the
same way as the other top wall plates.

LINTEL
2" x 4"

The door lintel also forms the
front top wall plate and, in
addition, serves as roof plate –
i.e., roof support. Any rafters
or cross beams can be attached
directly to any top wall plate.

Corner
upright

FRONT END OF THE TREE HOUSE

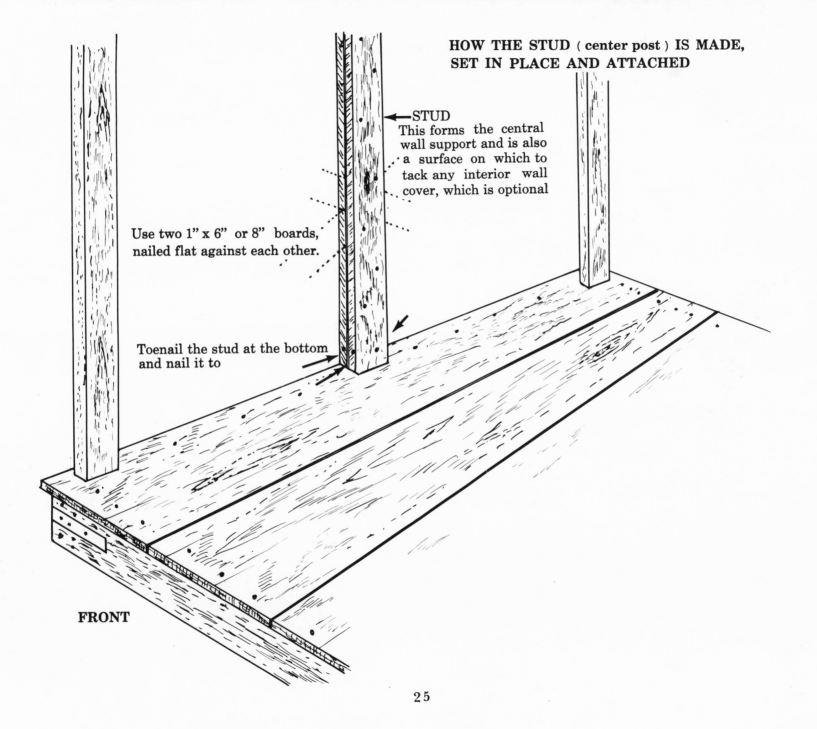

HOW THE STUD (center post) IS MADE, SET IN PLACE AND ATTACHED

←STUD
This forms the central wall support and is also a surface on which to tack any interior wall cover, which is optional

Use two 1" x 6" or 8" boards, nailed flat against each other.

Toenail the stud at the bottom and nail it to

FRONT

25

HOW THE STUD CROSSES THE DIAGONAL BRACES

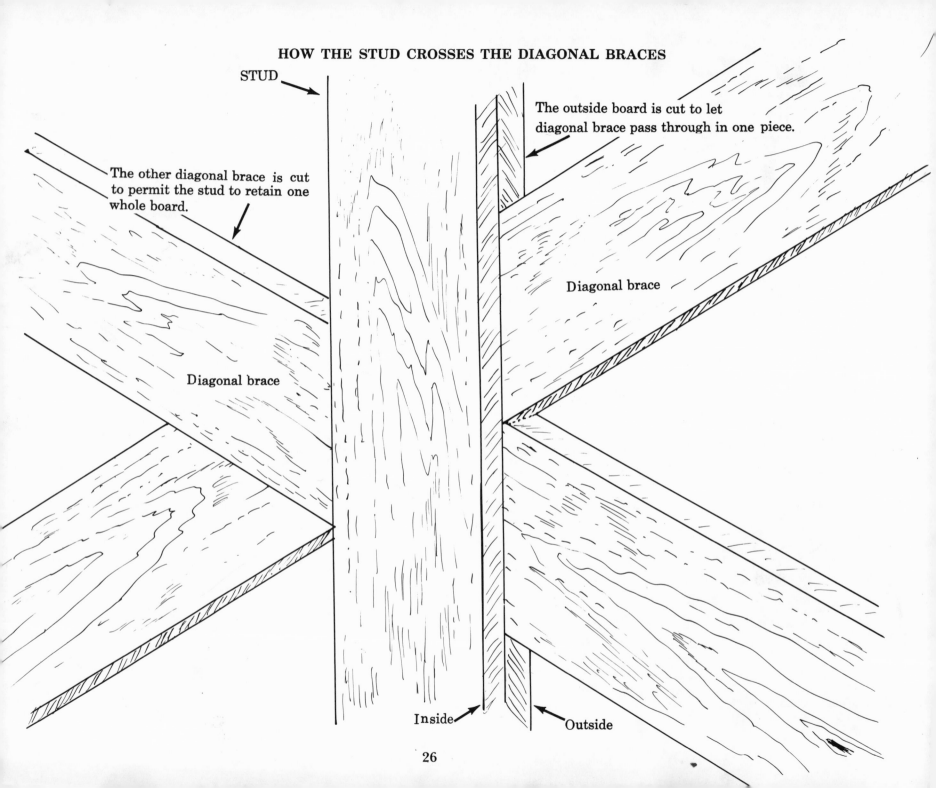

STUD

The outside board is cut to let diagonal brace pass through in one piece.

The other diagonal brace is cut to permit the stud to retain one whole board.

Diagonal brace

Diagonal brace

Diagonal brace

Inside

Outside

26

How Top Plates and Diagonals Fit to Uprights

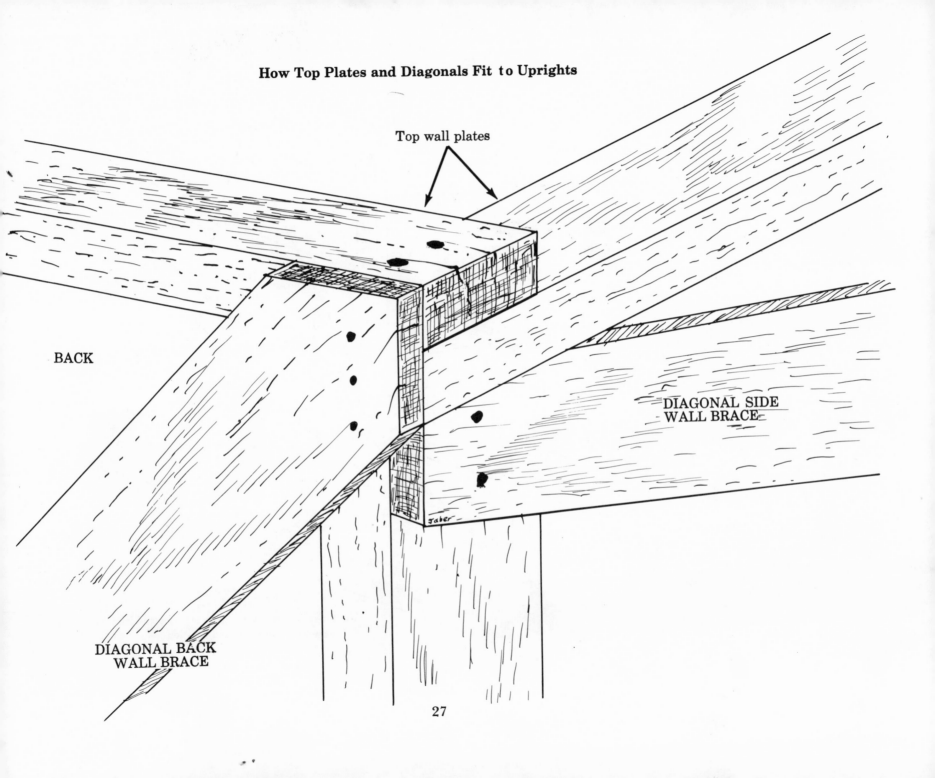

Top wall plates

BACK

DIAGONAL SIDE
WALL BRACE

DIAGONAL BACK
WALL BRACE

ADDING SIDE WALL DIAGONAL BRACES
AND TOP WALL PLATE

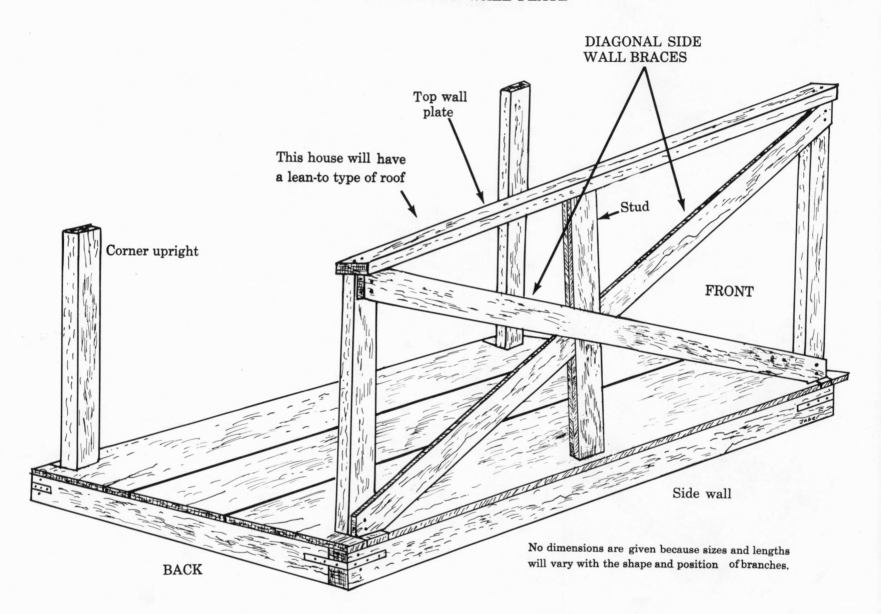

DIAGONAL SIDE
WALL BRACES

Top wall
plate

This house will have
a lean-to type of roof

Stud

Corner upright

FRONT

Side wall

BACK

No dimensions are given because sizes and lengths
will vary with the shape and position of branches.

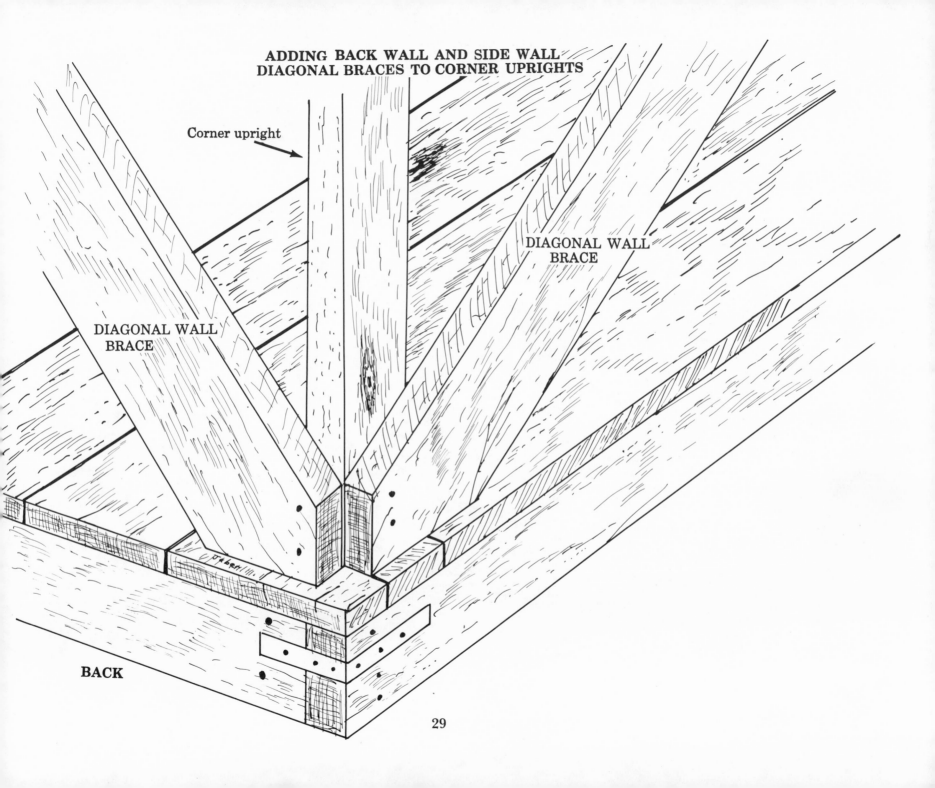

ADDING BACK WALL AND SIDE WALL
DIAGONAL BRACES TO CORNER UPRIGHTS

Corner upright

DIAGONAL WALL
BRACE

DIAGONAL WALL
BRACE

BACK

29

HOW THE BACK WALL AND SIDE WALL FRAMES
SHOULD LOOK WHEN ATTACHED TO THE PLATFORM

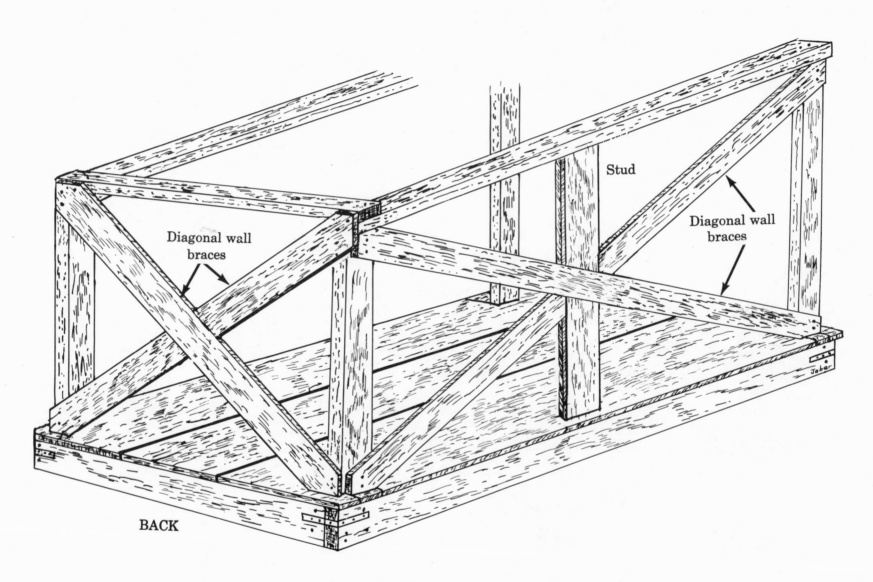

Diagonal wall braces

Stud

Diagonal wall braces

BACK

INTERIOR WALL FRAMEWORK

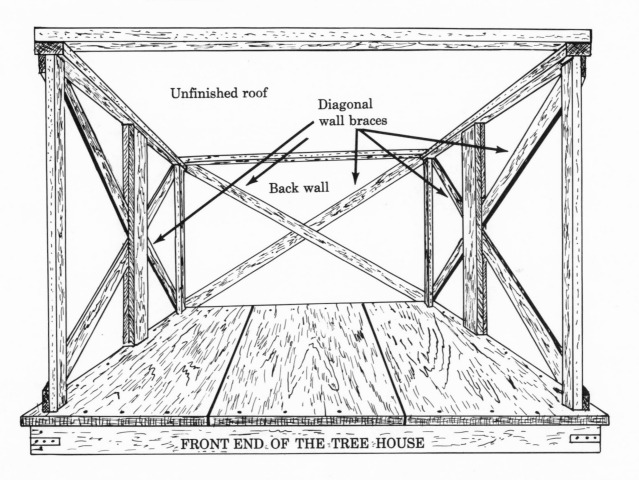

Unfinished roof

Diagonal
wall braces

Back wall

FRONT END OF THE TREE HOUSE

Doorway

31

WALL FRAMEWORK COMPLETED AND
READY FOR INTERIOR SURFACE COVERING

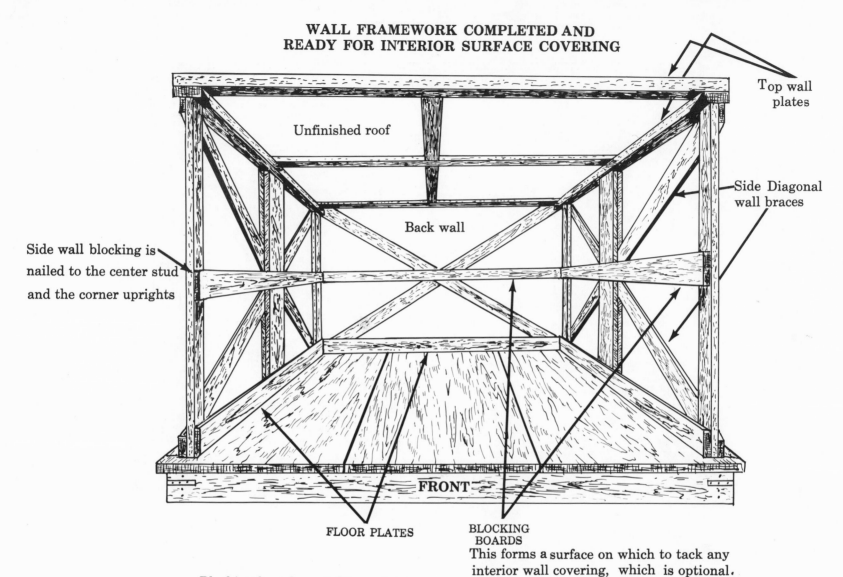

Top wall plates

Side Diagonal wall braces

Unfinished roof

Back wall

Side wall blocking is nailed to the center stud and the corner uprights

FRONT

FLOOR PLATES

BLOCKING BOARDS

This forms a surface on which to tack any interior wall covering, which is optional.

Blocking boards and Floor plates are nailed to uprights

In this house the wall's framework is designed to permit covering the interior, exterior or both. Blocking boards have to be added on the exterior wall if that is to be covered.

32

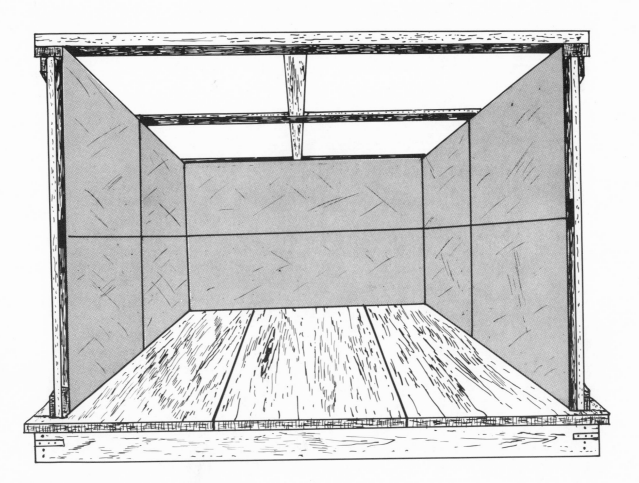

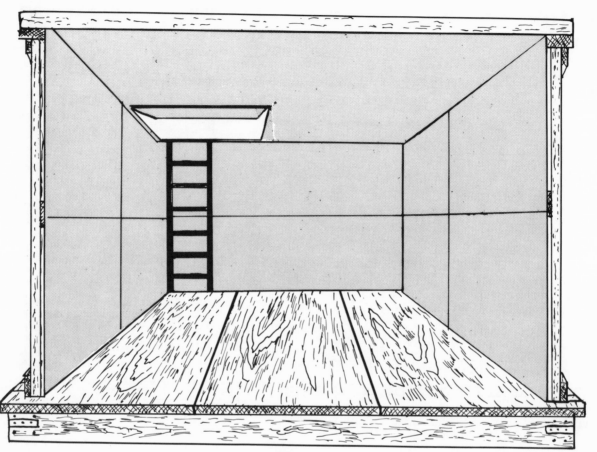

34

ADDING THE DOOR

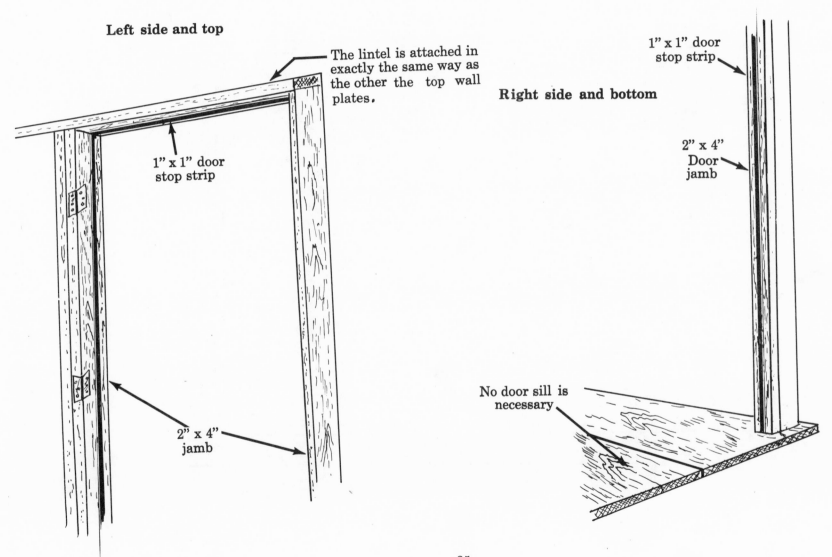

Left side and top

The lintel is attached in exactly the same way as the other the top wall plates.

1" x 1" door stop strip

2" x 4" jamb

Right side and bottom

1" x 1" door stop strip

2" x 4" Door jamb

No door sill is necessary

FRONT FRAMEWORK COMPLETED

Framework in front to make a window and a door

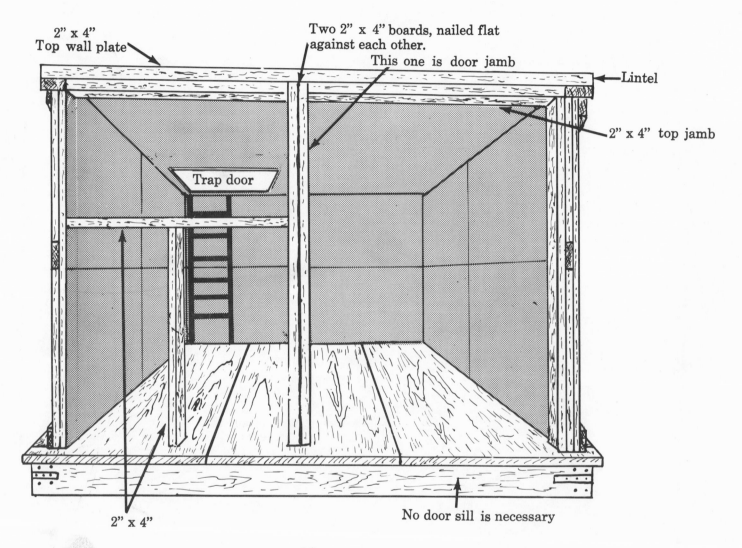

2" x 4"
Top wall plate

Two 2" x 4" boards, nailed flat
against each other.
This one is door jamb

Lintel

2" x 4" top jamb

Trap door

2" x 4"

No door sill is necessary

HOW THE DOOR IS MADE

If boards are to be used instead of plywood, build a simple batten door

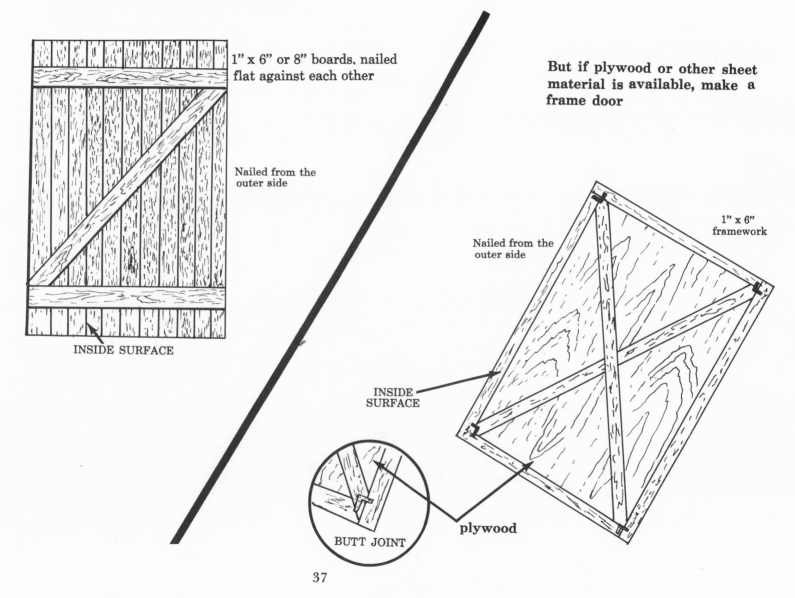

1" x 6" or 8" boards, nailed flat against each other

Nailed from the outer side

INSIDE SURFACE

But if plywood or other sheet material is available, make a frame door

1" x 6" framework

Nailed from the outer side

INSIDE SURFACE

BUTT JOINT

plywood

THE COMPLETED FRONT WITH WINDOW
AND DOOR

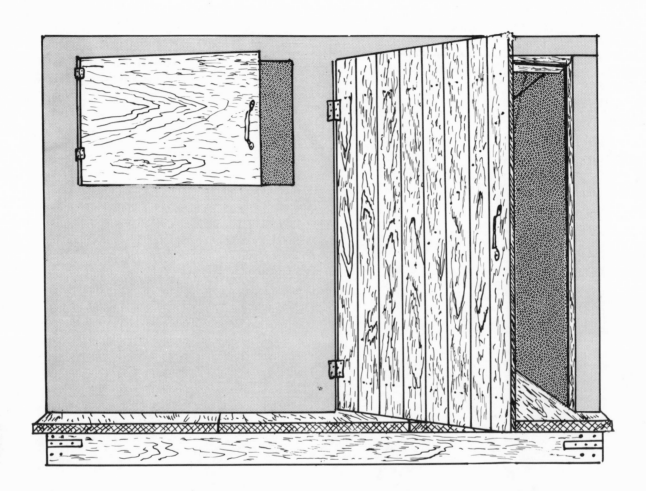

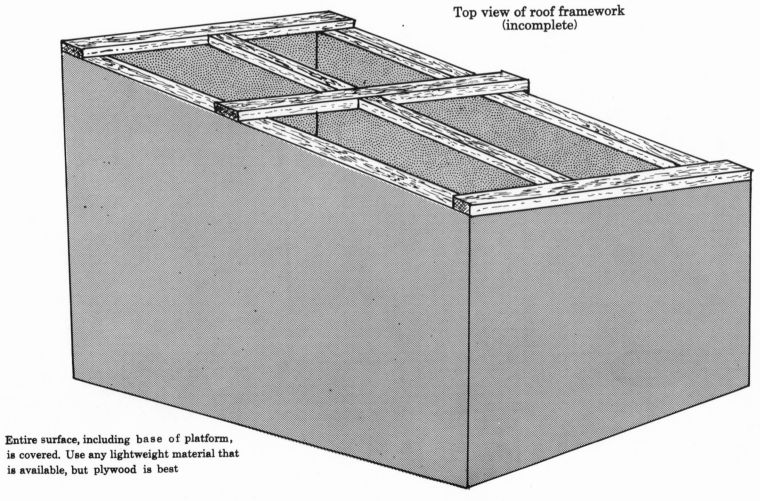

Top view of roof framework
(incomplete)

Entire surface, including base of platform,
is covered. Use any lightweight material that
is available, but plywood is best

COMPLETING THE ROOF FRAMEWORK

Top view of roof framework
(complete)

2" x 4"
roof

CEILING JOIST
2" x 4"

The roof plates are used to
support rafters , cross beams
or covering

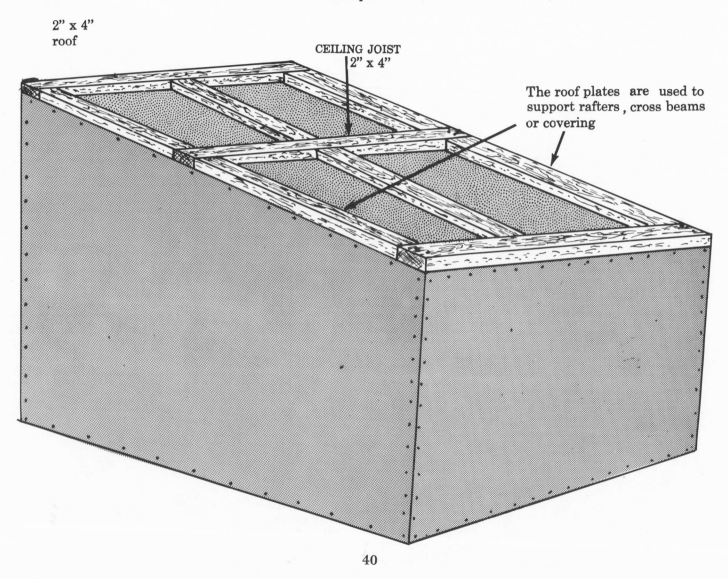

ADDING ROOFING BOARDS AND COVER

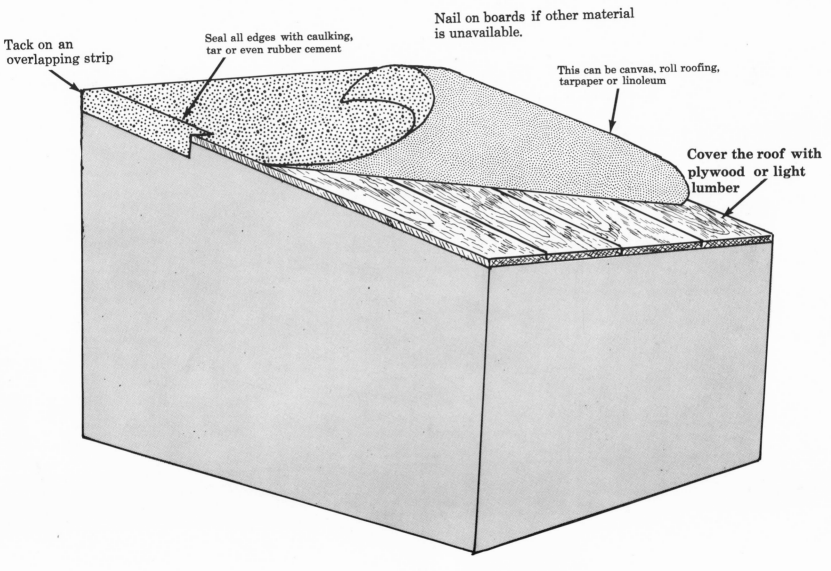

Tack on an overlapping strip

Seal all edges with caulking, tar or even rubber cement

Nail on boards if other material is unavailable.

This can be canvas, roll roofing, tarpaper or linoleum

Cover the roof with plywood or light lumber

41

THE COMPLETED TREE HOUSE
REAR VIEW

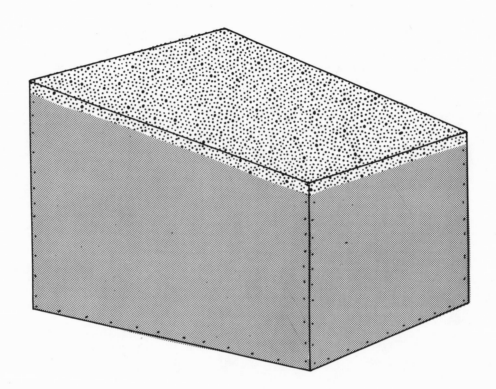

42

PLANNING A WINDOW

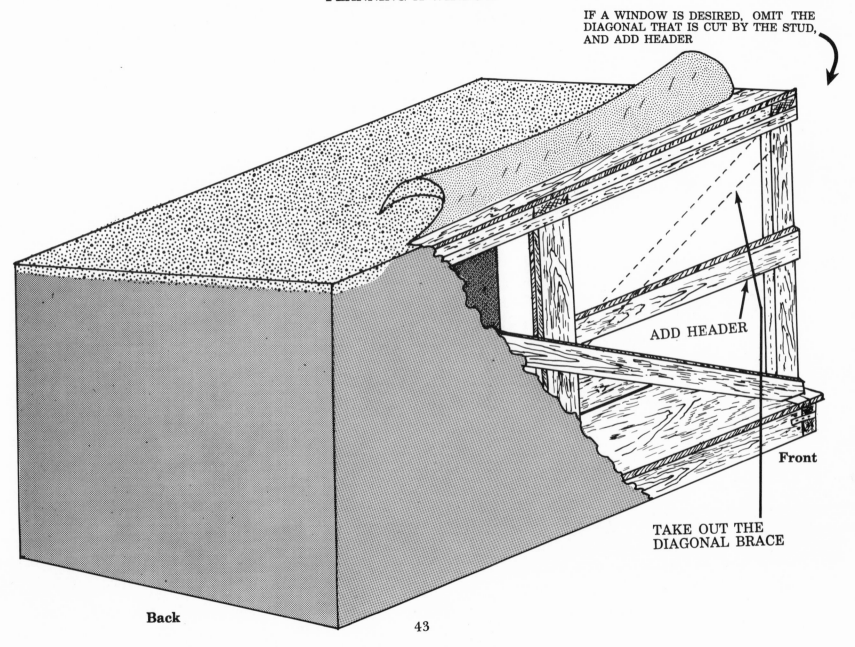

IF A WINDOW IS DESIRED, OMIT THE DIAGONAL THAT IS CUT BY THE STUD, AND ADD HEADER

ADD HEADER

Front

TAKE OUT THE DIAGONAL BRACE

Back

43

MAKING A HINGED WINDOW COVER

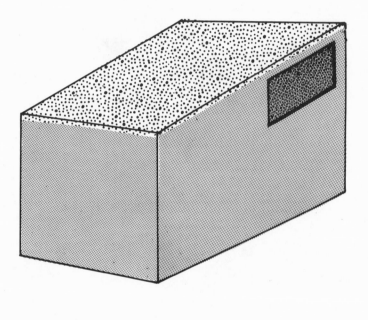

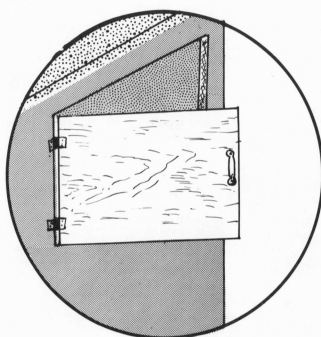

44

AN OBSERVATION DECK

Reached by trap door through the roof

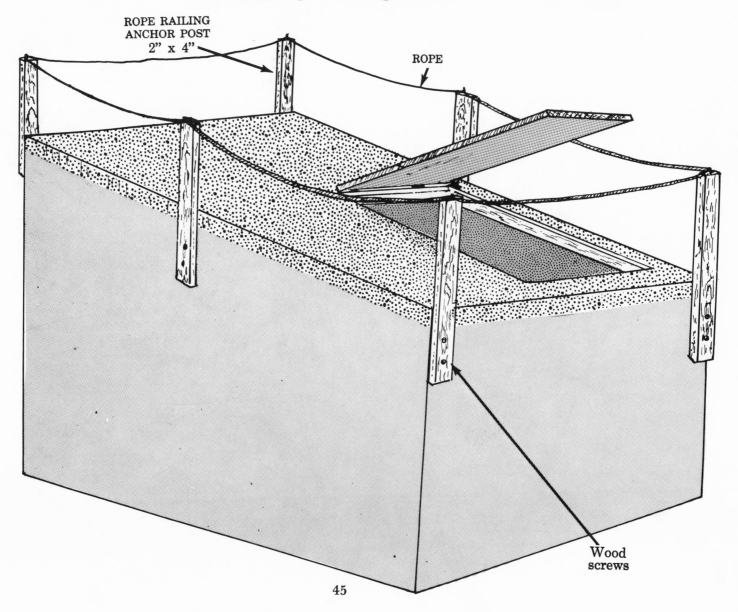

ROPE RAILING
ANCHOR POST
2" x 4"

ROPE

Wood
screws

45

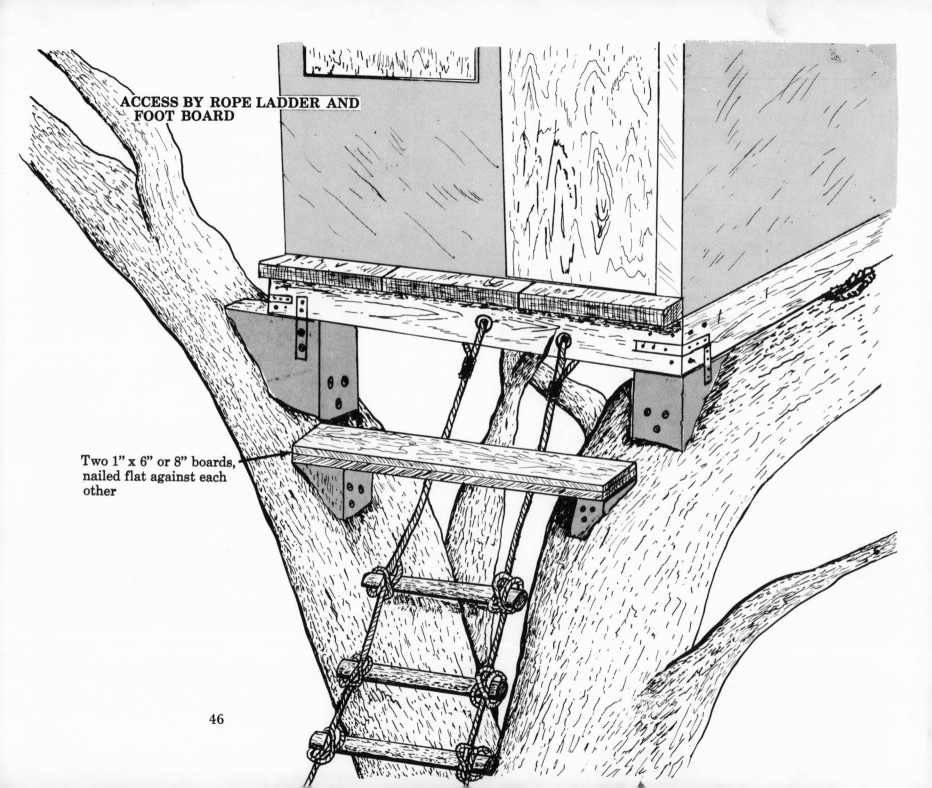

ACCESS BY ROPE LADDER AND FOOT BOARD

Two 1" x 6" or 8" boards, nailed flat against each other

46

THE TREE HOUSE COMPLETED

47

A gable house has to be planned from the start.
All corner uprights have to be the same length,
and no ceiling joists are necessary. But the roof
plates must remain. No roof struts are needed,
unless heavy boards are being used for covering.

The roof plates
must remain

No ceiling joists

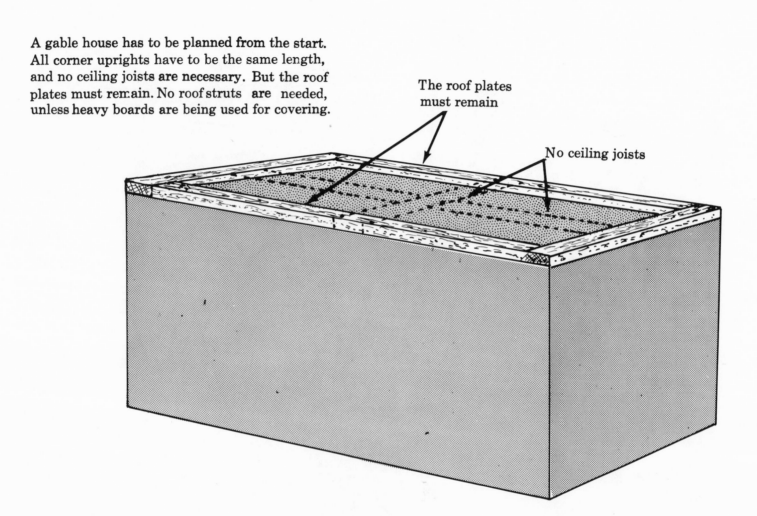

THE GABLE ROOF FRAMEWORK

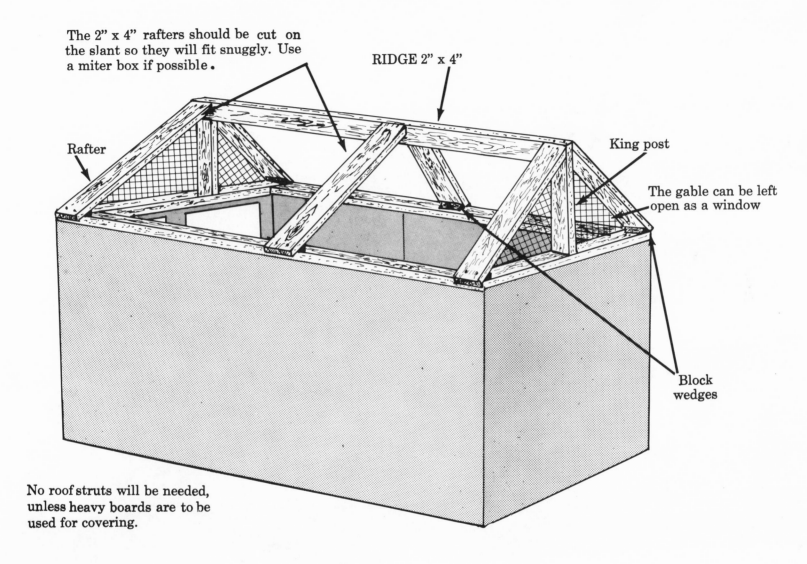

The 2" x 4" rafters should be cut on the slant so they will fit snuggly. Use a miter box if possible.

RIDGE 2" x 4"

Rafter

King post

The gable can be left open as a window

Block wedges

No roof struts will be needed, unless heavy boards are to be used for covering.

THE COMPLETED GABLE ROOF

**Cover the roof with plywood
or light lumber**

The cover can be any lightweight
material that is available, even canvas,
roll roofing, tarpaper or linoleum

Join above
the ridge

The gable can be left
open as a window

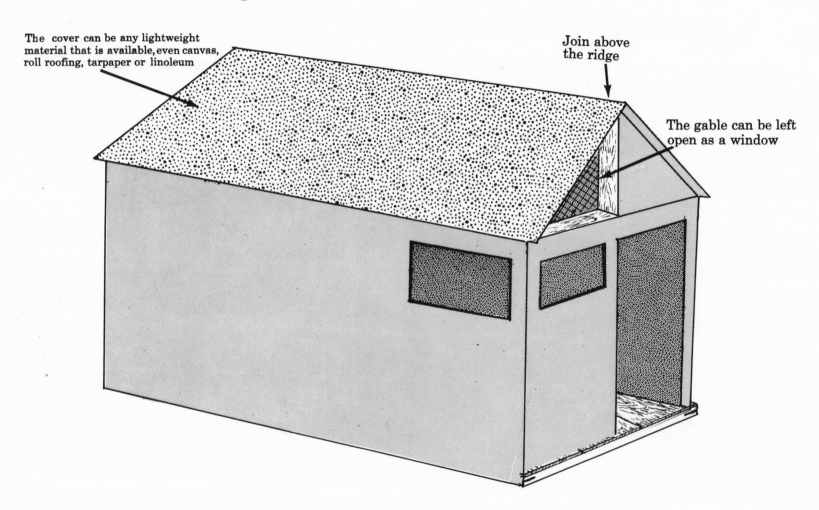

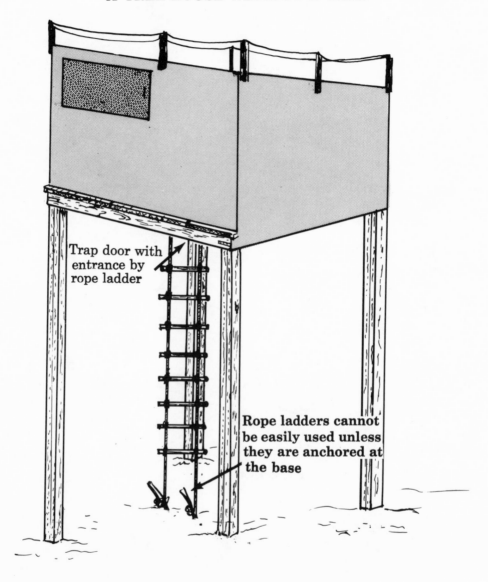

Trap door with
entrance by
rope ladder

Rope ladders cannot
be easily used unless
they are anchored at
the base

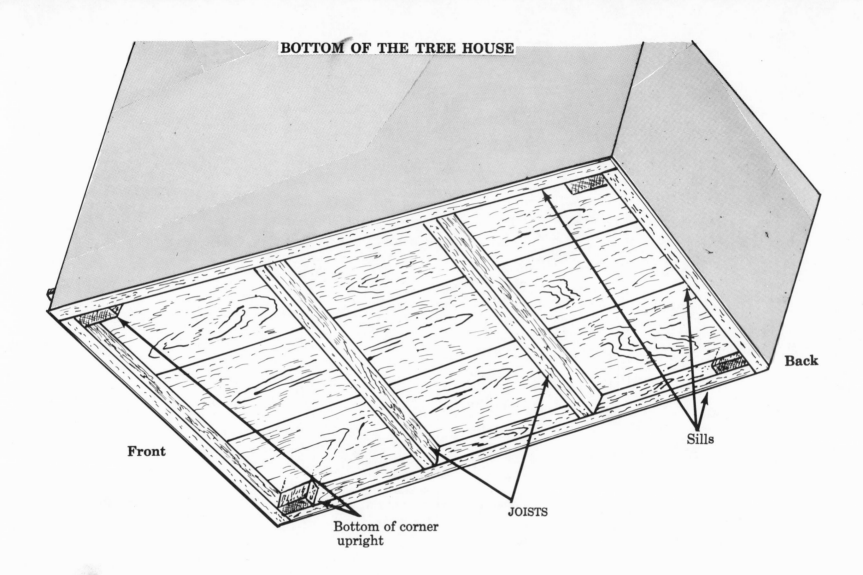

BOTTOM OF THE TREE HOUSE

Front

Back

Sills

JOISTS

Bottom of corner
upright

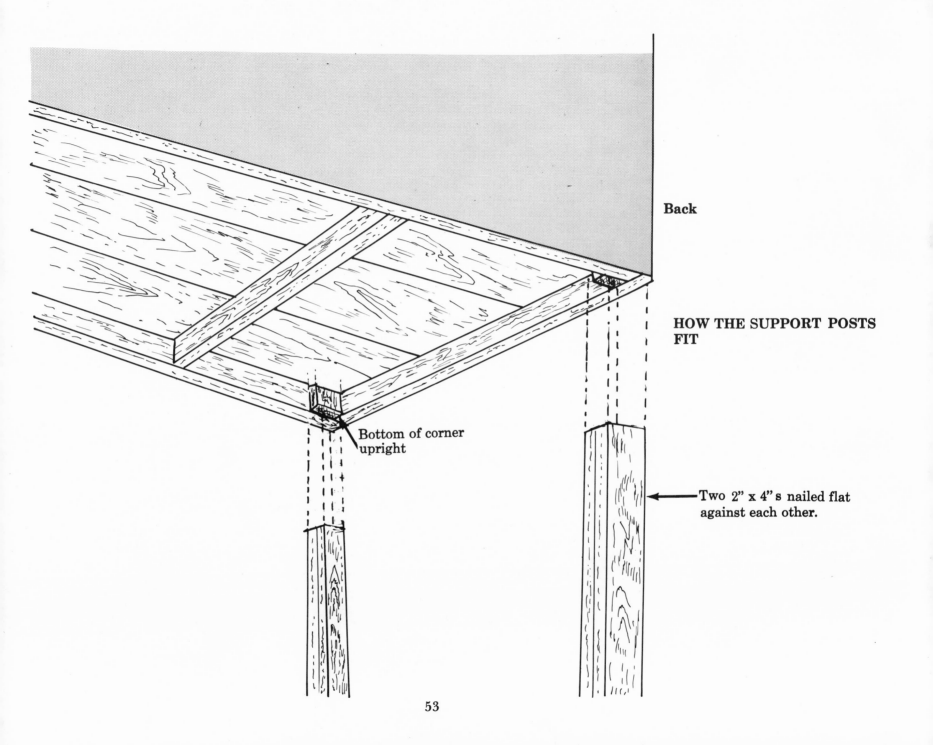

Back

HOW THE SUPPORT POSTS FIT

Bottom of corner upright

Two 2" x 4" s nailed flat against each other.

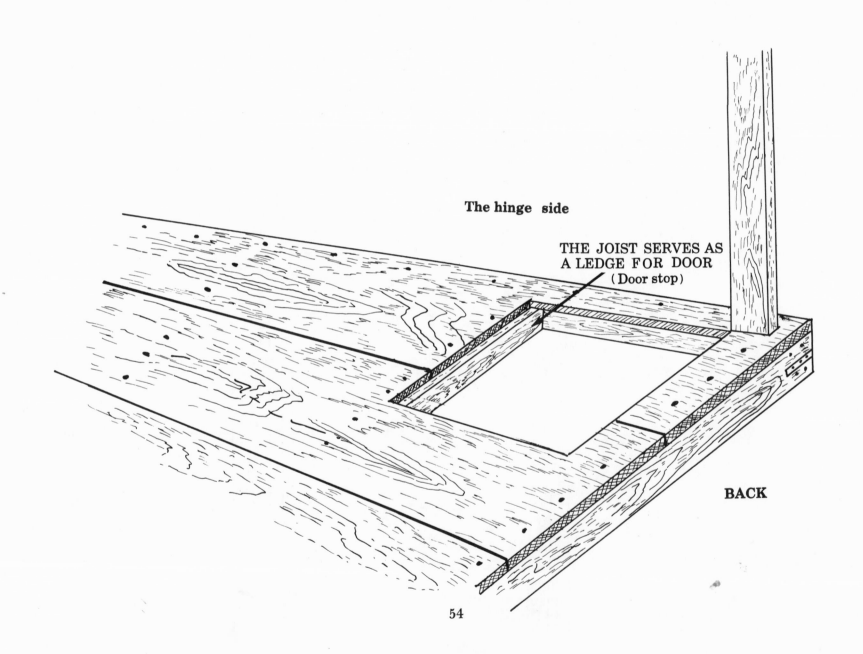

The hinge side

THE JOIST SERVES AS
A LEDGE FOR DOOR
(Door stop)

BACK

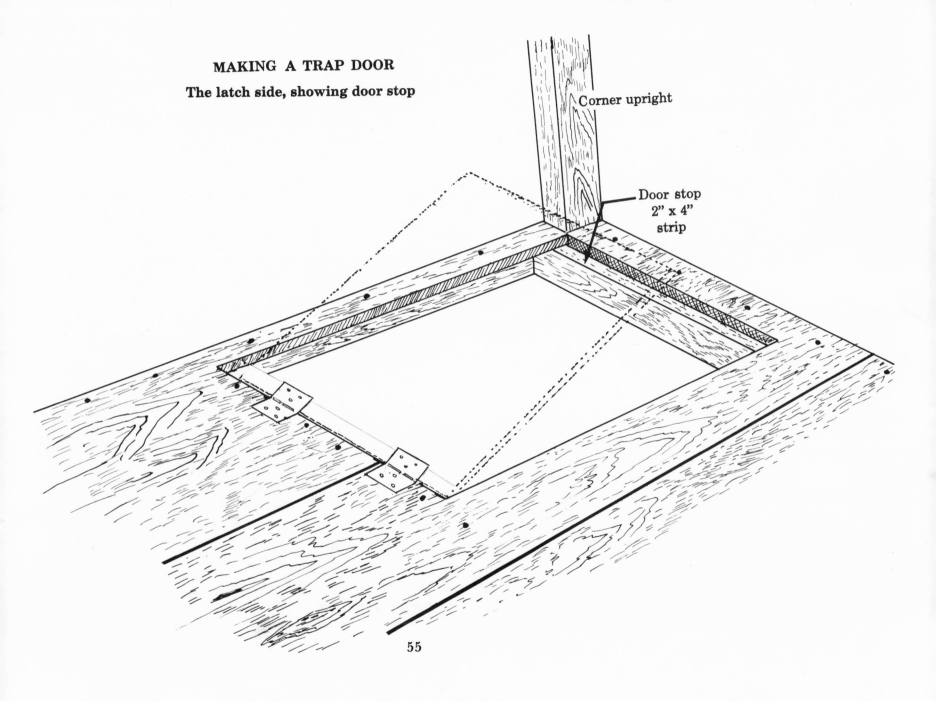

MAKING A TRAP DOOR

The latch side, showing door stop

Corner upright

Door stop
2" x 4"
strip

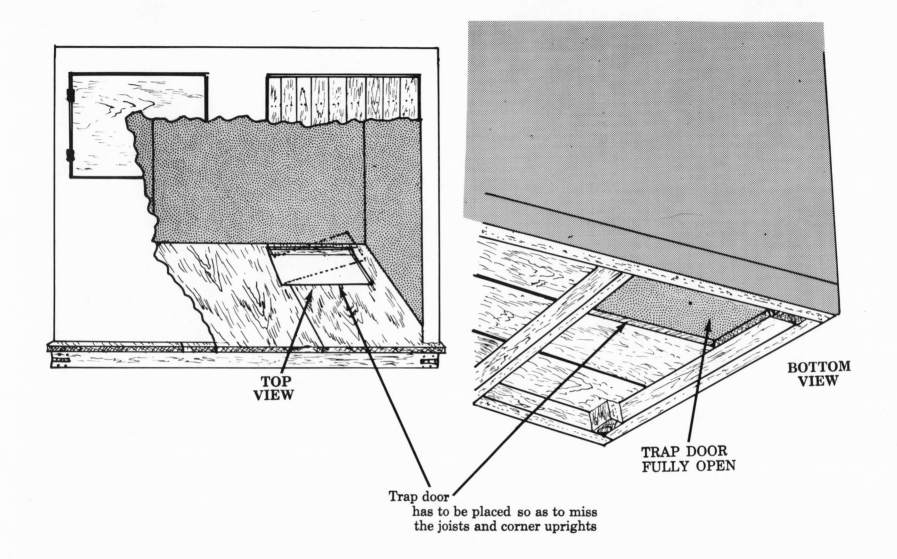

TOP
VIEW

BOTTOM
VIEW

TRAP DOOR
FULLY OPEN

Trap door
has to be placed so as to miss
the joists and corner uprights

PLANNING A TRAP DOOR IN THE FLOOR

56

USING A LIVE TREE TRUNK AS A SUPPORT POST

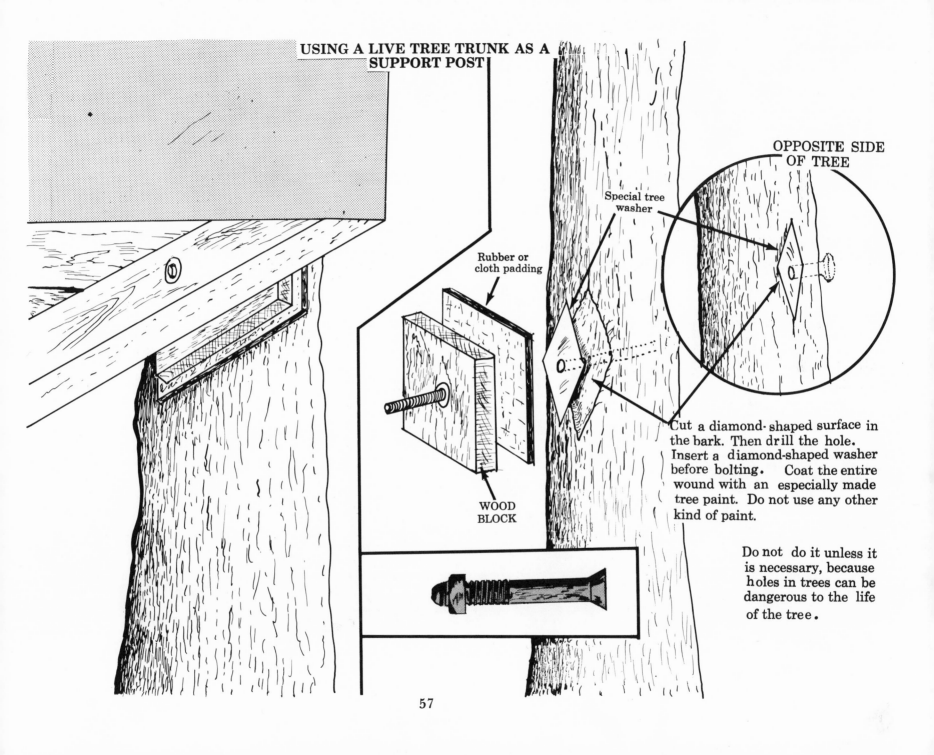

OPPOSITE SIDE OF TREE

Special tree washer

Rubber or cloth padding

WOOD BLOCK

Cut a diamond-shaped surface in the bark. Then drill the hole. Insert a diamond-shaped washer before bolting. Coat the entire wound with an especially made tree paint. Do not use any other kind of paint.

Do not do it unless it is necessary, because holes in trees can be dangerous to the life of the tree.

HOW TO MAKE A ROPE LADDER

Two types of hitches are needed: one to lash the ladder rope to a branch or beam and the other to form the ladder.

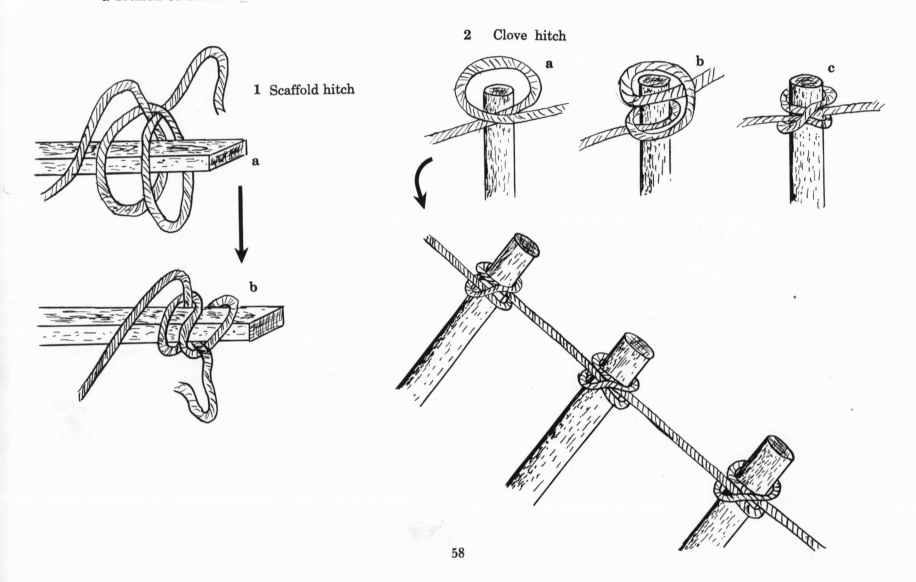

1 Scaffold hitch

2 Clove hitch

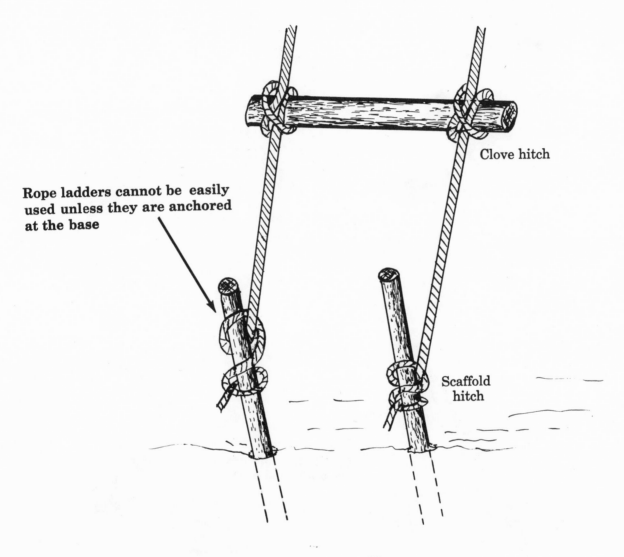

Clove hitch

Rope ladders cannot be easily
used unless they are anchored
at the base

Scaffold
hitch

A TREE SEAT

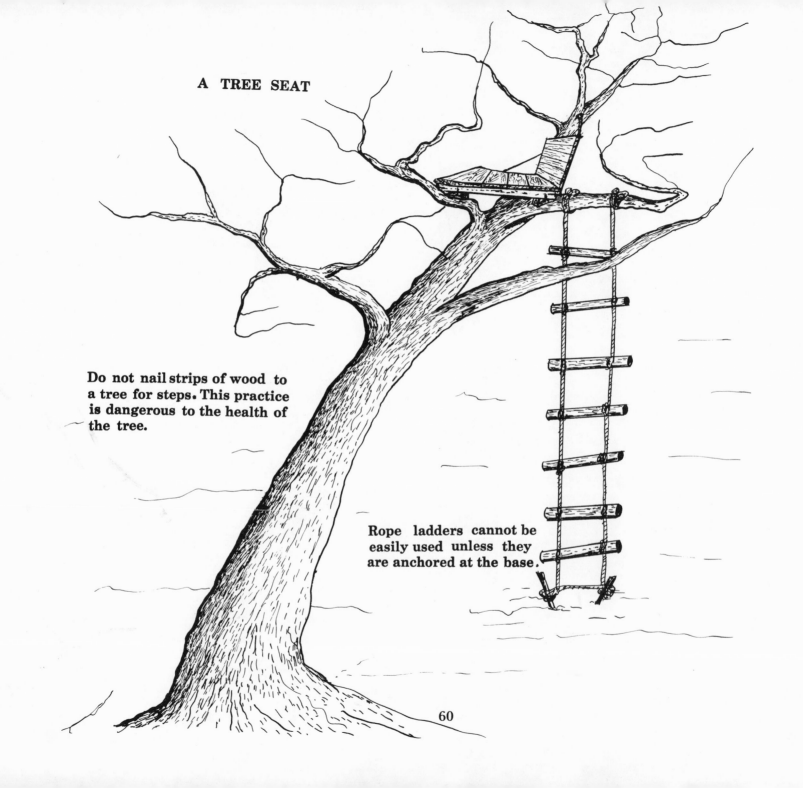

Do not nail strips of wood to a tree for steps. This practice is dangerous to the health of the tree.

Rope ladders cannot be easily used unless they are anchored at the base.

60

BUILDING A TREE SEAT

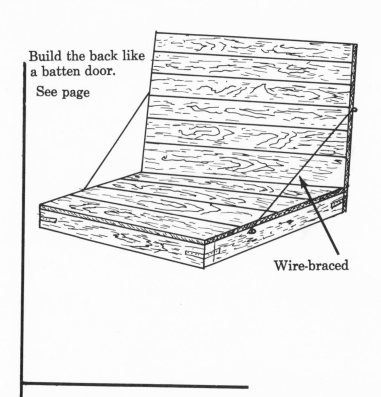

Build the back like a batten door.

See page

Wire-braced

The seat bottom is constructed exactly like the tree house platform, and is attached in the same manner.

Reverse side of seat back

62

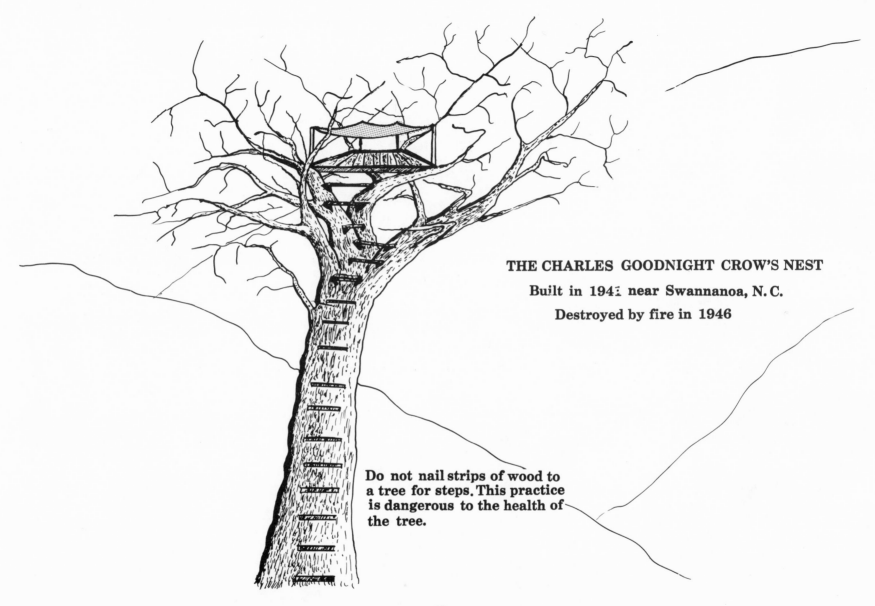

THE CHARLES GOODNIGHT CROW'S NEST

Built in 1941 near Swannanoa, N.C.

Destroyed by fire in 1946

Do not nail strips of wood to a tree for steps. This practice is dangerous to the health of the tree.

63

A high-set, half-suspended tree house

A tree house that was built in a black oak in 1931 at Monclova, Ohio, near Toledo. It no longer exists.

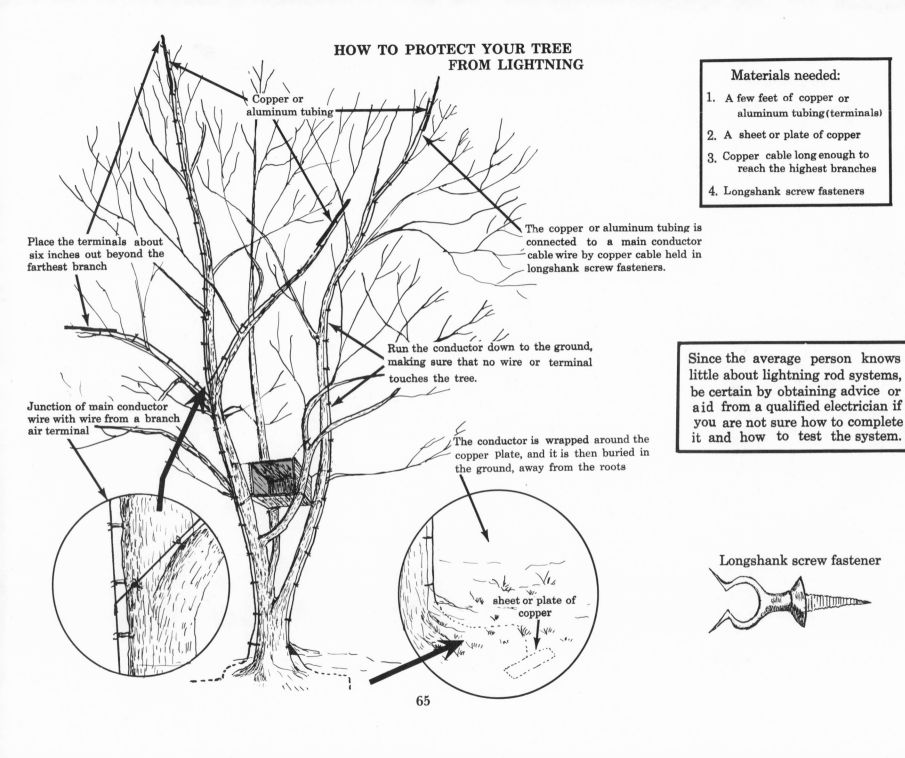

HOW TO PROTECT YOUR TREE FROM LIGHTNING

Copper or aluminum tubing

Materials needed:

1. A few feet of copper or aluminum tubing (terminals)
2. A sheet or plate of copper
3. Copper cable long enough to reach the highest branches
4. Longshank screw fasteners

The copper or aluminum tubing is connected to a main conductor cable wire by copper cable held in longshank screw fasteners.

Place the terminals about six inches out beyond the farthest branch

Run the conductor down to the ground, making sure that no wire or terminal touches the tree.

Junction of main conductor wire with wire from a branch air terminal

The conductor is wrapped around the copper plate, and it is then buried in the ground, away from the roots

Since the average person knows little about lightning rod systems, be certain by obtaining advice or aid from a qualified electrician if you are not sure how to complete it and how to test the system.

sheet or plate of copper

Longshank screw fastener

65

HOW TO CABLE-BRACE A TREE

To prevent a split in the crotch, or to help support a weak crotch

Since your tree house is to be attached on and between trunks or large branches, the direction of pressure is outward, putting added strain on limb and trunk crotches. You may find it necessary to cable-brace the tree. But do not do it unless it is necessary, because holes in trees can be dangerous to the life of the tree.

Materials needed: Two eyebolts; Heavy, three-strand cable; Diamond-shaped washer, A brace with a bit exactly the size of the eyebolt

 Eyebolt

Thimble   Thimbles can be purchased at hardware stores.

1   2   3

Make an eye in the cable

Use a thimble (eyepiece) to prevent rapid wearing on the cable.

Diamond-shaped washer

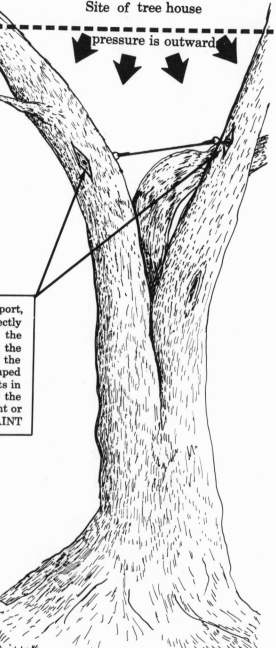

Site of tree house

pressure is outward

To minimize the strain and give added support, drill a hole in both limbs or trunks directly opposite each other at the points where the eyebolts will be inserted.   Make the hole the same diameter as the eyebolt. Cut away the bark around each to form a diamond - shaped slit.   Use a diamond-shaped washer that fits in the slit and over the bolt, and then tighten the nut. Finally, paint the wound with tree paint or shellac.   DO NOT USE HOUSEHOLD PAINT

Do not use eyebolts to cable small branches. Lag screws are better.

Lag screw

66

TREE INJURY

What to do if you accidentally tear off tree bark or cut into the living wood

With a sharp knife, cut away any loose bark.   Then cut and shape the wound, exposing a diamond-shaped surface of the sapwood.   Coat the entire wound with tree paint.   It is especially made for trees.   Do not use any other kind of paint.   The coating of tree paint keeps out disease-causing organisms and prevents decay. In time , the wound will be covered by new bark.

How to keep crawling insects from climbing the tree and in - vading the tree house

Apply a mixture of cotton and glue in a band as wide as

a strip of flypaper. Lay flypaper over the band.

Some garden supply centers sell an adhesive

especially made for this purpose

Do not leave this material on the tree permanently—it can cause bark decay. Bark protects the tree from disease.

67

IF YOU MUST LOP OFF A BRANCH
Here is the proper way to do it

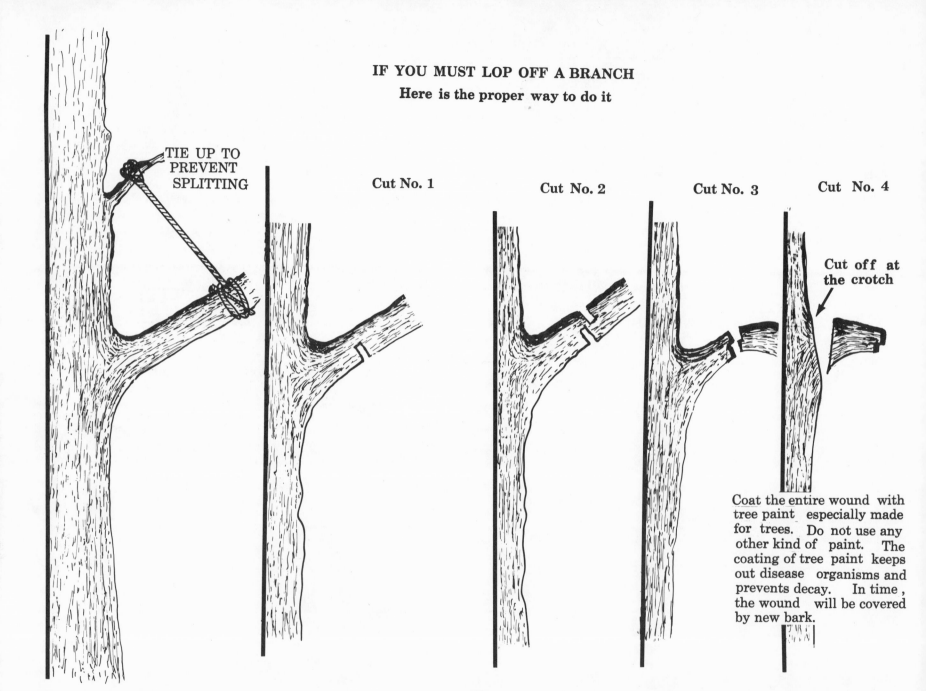

TIE UP TO PREVENT SPLITTING

Cut No. 1

Cut No. 2

Cut No. 3

Cut No. 4

Cut off at the crotch

Coat the entire wound with tree paint especially made for trees. Do not use any other kind of paint. The coating of tree paint keeps out disease organisms and prevents decay. In time, the wound will be covered by new bark.

TIPS ON HOW TO PREVENT INJURIES TO YOURSELF
AND OTHERS WHILE BUILDING A TREE HOUSE

Check for dead branches, and remove them by sawing them off right at their bases. Then paint
the wounds with special tree paint. See page

Avoid working in a tree near electric wires.   Do not leave tools in a tree.

Be sure that your ladder is safe.   Watch out for poison ivy. See page 70

Use a safety belt when working on high-set platforms, or when working up in the tree at the trunk.

Always be on the lookout for poison ivy. Its leaves are a glossy green in summer, but become
reddish in autumn.   The leaves grow in clusters of three, and the plant often grows up trunks
of trees.

Certain materials, such as asbestos boards, and plate glass should not be used unless you have ex-
perience with them.

DO NOT REMAIN IN OR NEAR ANY TREE DURING A RAIN OR THUNDERSHOWER

Keep small children away, and children under seven should never be permitted in a tree house.

See page 70

Warning

Tools such as axes and hatchets look easy
to use, but in fact a lot of skill is required
to use them safely.   The placing of the
hands and feet while cutting are important,
and so is the direction and angle of each cut.

When chopping with an axe, keep the feet
back and apart --lean forward.   Do not use
the foot to hold or steady the piece you are
cutting unless you are an expert in the art of
chopping.

The same advice applies to the hands when splitting
or chopping with a hatchet.

Certian materials, such as sheet
glass, and asbestos, should not
be used in the tree house.

Do not use razor blades for cutting on wood
They may snap off to injure the user. There
are many especially designed tools for this
purpose, such as wood chisels, scrapers,
planes, spokeshaves, awls and rasps. All of
these are safer to use.

WATCH OUT FOR POISON IVY and POISON OAK

Always be on the lookout for poison ivy. Its leaves are a glossy green in summer, but become reddish in autumn. The leaves grow in clusters of three, and the plant often grows up trunks of trees. Identification of poison ivy may be difficult, because its leaves vary in size and shape, and it also looks a lot like the harmless Virginia creeper.

Poison ivy looks like this:

All six of these are varieties of poison ivy

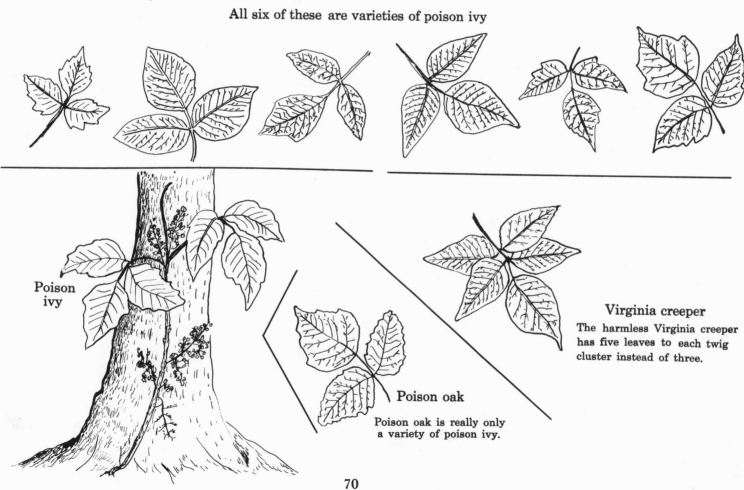

Poison ivy

Poison oak

Poison oak is really only a variety of poison ivy.

Virginia creeper

The harmless Virginia creeper has five leaves to each twig cluster instead of three.

FOR SMALL CHILDREN ONLY

Let us give small children a chance to paly together, safely

Small children should not be permitted to play in a tree house built and situated in the manner described up to this point in the book. Instead, it is recommended that a multipurpose house be built for their own especial use. It can be constructed in a manner that allows a child free expression of his or her imagination. The child should be able to visualize the structure as a tree house, a ship's deck, the deck of a raft, an island, or other secure private playing surface. But in order for it to be a safe playing area, the structure must be built carefully, to give the impression of height without actually being more than a few feet off the ground. Any sort of deck surface on the structure should be protected with heavy railings, and access should not be by ladder, but by a secure and solid set of stairs, equipped with handrails. All wood surfaces have to be smooth finished, and any sharp projections must be avoided in the construction features. Headroom should be exaggerated, and all lintels should be padded. With these precautions in mind, let us start with the platform, which is to include the deck surface.

MAKING DECK AND FLOORING PLATFORM

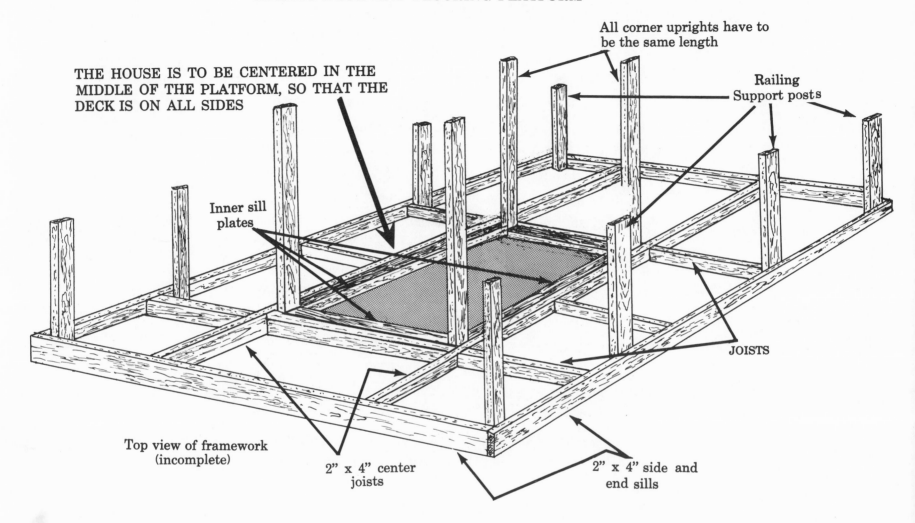

All corner uprights have to be the same length

Railing
Support posts

THE HOUSE IS TO BE CENTERED IN THE MIDDLE OF THE PLATFORM, SO THAT THE DECK IS ON ALL SIDES

Inner sill plates

JOISTS

Top view of framework (incomplete)

2" x 4" center joists

2" x 4" side and end sills

72

HOUSE FRAME and FLOOR NEARLY COMPLETED
With railing and corner uprights in position

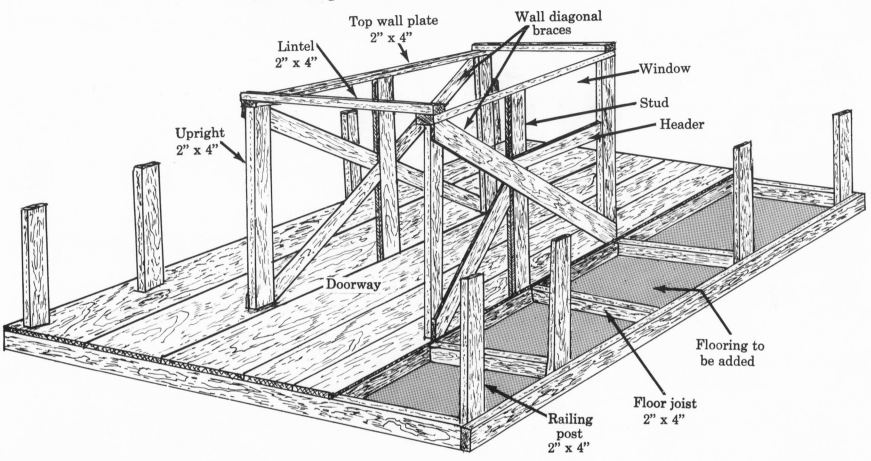

Top wall plate
2" x 4"

Wall diagonal braces

Lintel
2" x 4"

Window

Stud

Header

Upright
2" x 4"

Doorway

Flooring to
be added

Railing
post
2" x 4"

Floor joist
2" x 4"

NEARLY COMPLETE RAILING, DECK and HOUSE

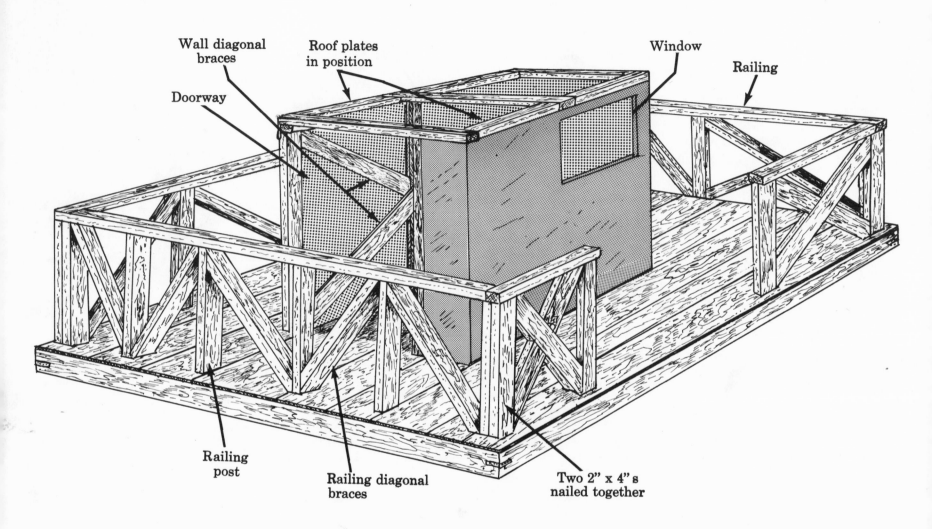

Wall diagonal braces

Roof plates in position

Window

Railing

Doorway

Railing post

Railing diagonal braces

Two 2" x 4" s nailed together

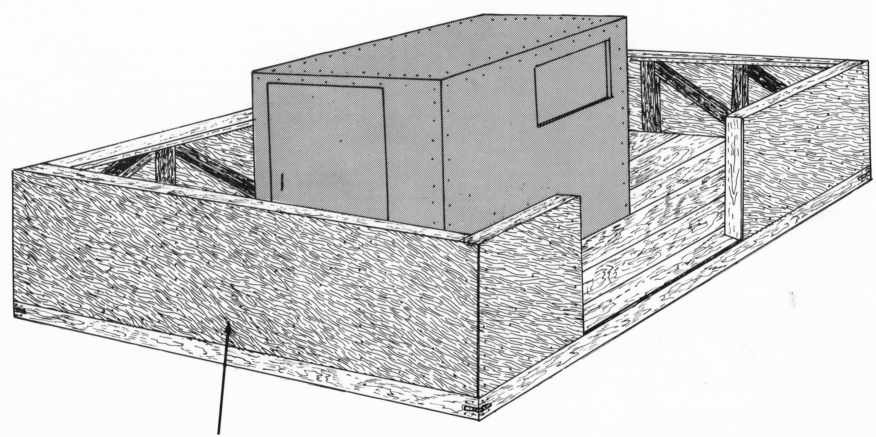

The outer covering of the railing is
optional, but it is safer for small children

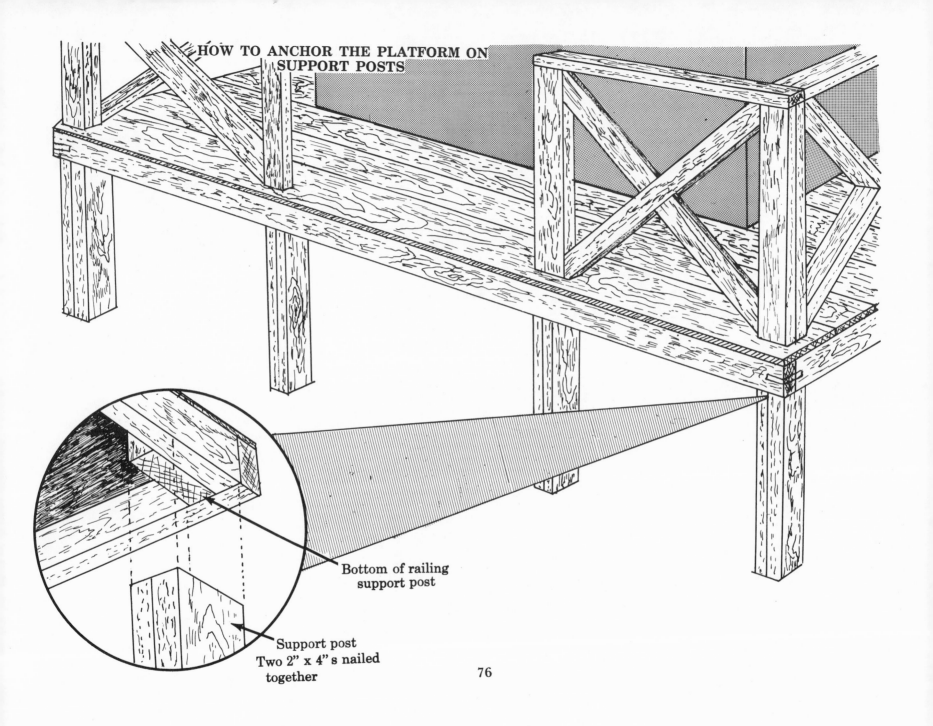

HOW TO ANCHOR THE PLATFORM ON SUPPORT POSTS

Bottom of railing
support post

Support post
Two 2" x 4"s nailed
together

76

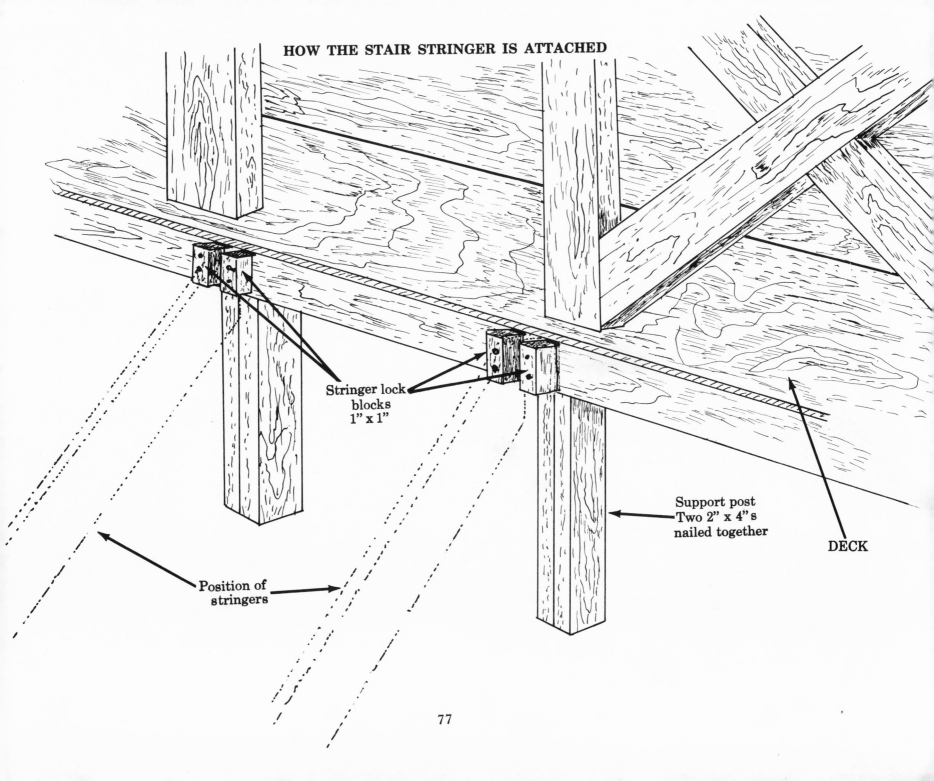

HOW THE STAIR STRINGER IS ATTACHED

Stringer lock
blocks
1" x 1"

Position of
stringers

Support post
Two 2" x 4"s
nailed together

DECK

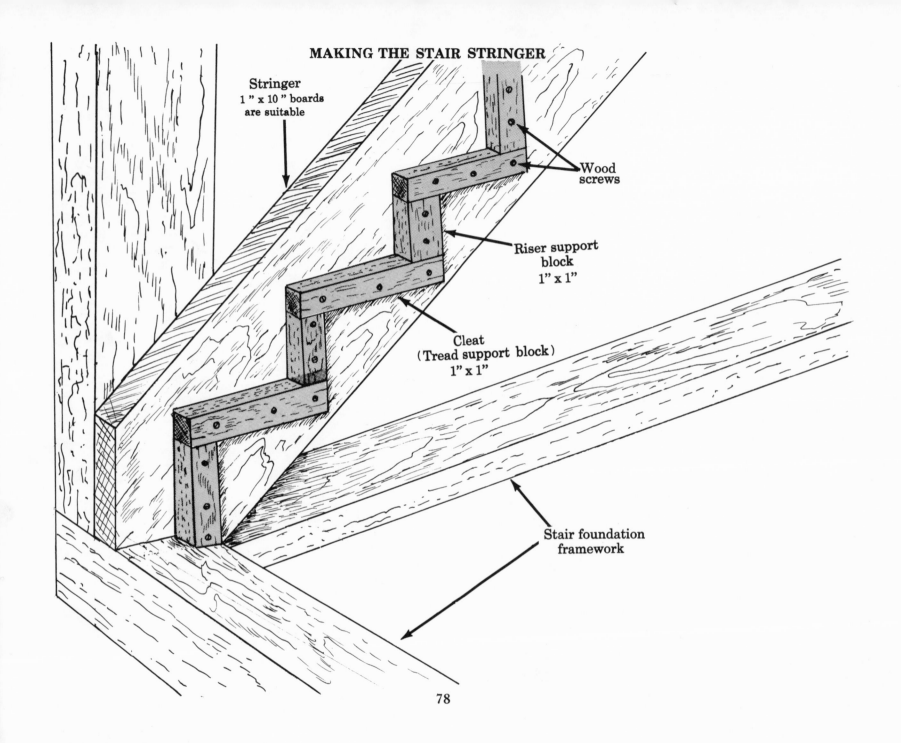

MAKING THE STAIR STRINGER

Stringer
1 " x 10 " boards
are suitable

Wood
screws

Riser support
block
1" x 1"

Cleat
(Tread support block)
1" x 1"

Stair foundation
framework

78

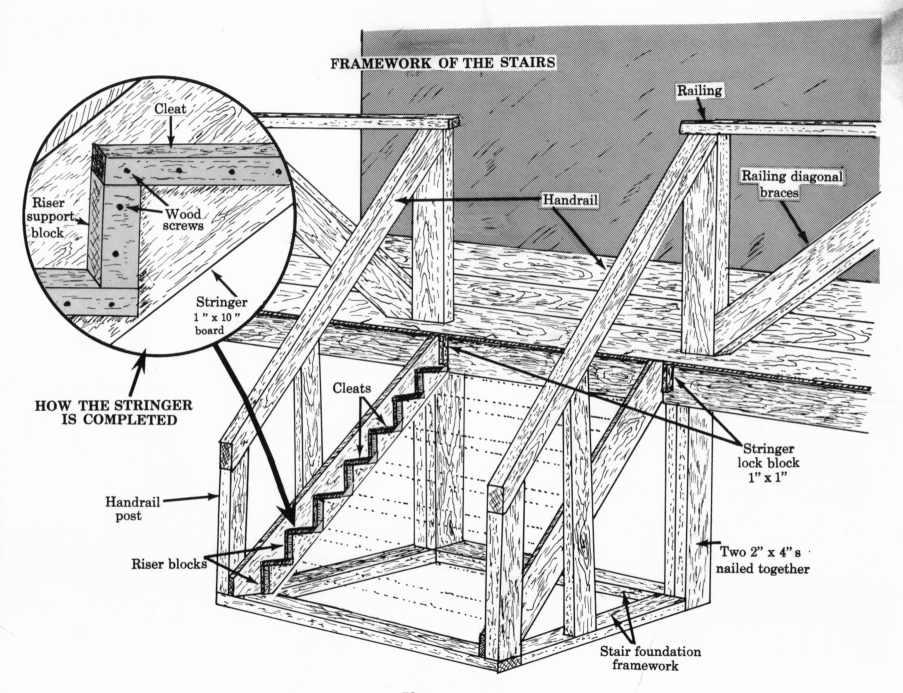

FRAMEWORK OF THE STAIRS

Cleat

Riser support block

Wood screws

Stringer 1" x 10" board

HOW THE STRINGER IS COMPLETED

Handrail post

Riser blocks

Cleats

Railing

Handrail

Railing diagonal braces

Stringer lock block 1" x 1"

Two 2" x 4"s nailed together

Stair foundation framework

THE COMPLETED STAIR

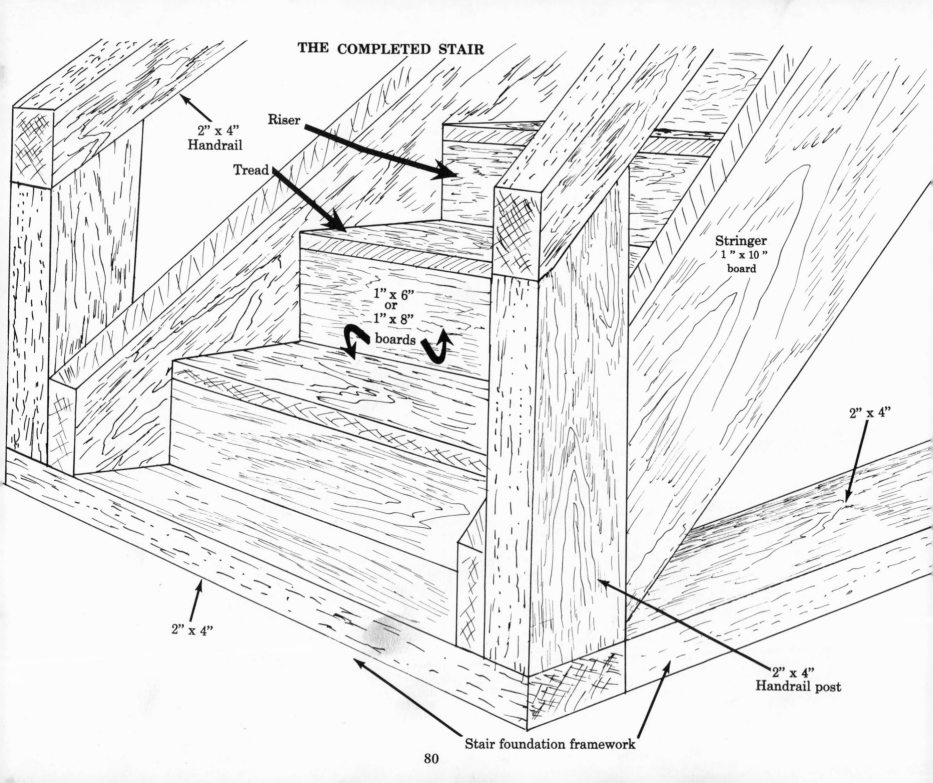

2" x 4"
Handrail

Riser

Tread

1" x 6"
or
1" x 8"
boards

Stringer
1 " x 10 "
board

2" x 4"

2" x 4"

2" x 4"
Handrail post

Stair foundation framework

THE MONOPOLY GAME TREE HOUSE OF BROOKVILLE, N. Y.

This is the tree house in which a record-breaking series of consecutive monopoly games was played.

It represents the combined efforts of seven young men of Brookville, New York.   The builders, John Vigliotti, Jim Winter, Richard Salz, Stewart Arnold, Roger Lanctot, Peter Knapp, and Bill Kulakowski were also the players.   The house is located on the Vigliotti property.   The surroundings are a serene and ideal place in which to build a tree house.   The house is supported by three live tree trunks.   A fourth point of contact with a tree   was unavailable for the square form, and so one corner is supported   by a   single   2" x 4" post.   The main framework is made up of 2" x 4" timber.   There   are a side entrance ,   two windows and a trap door to the roof.   The roof and floor are sturdy, but the house is not suitable for small children, since its mode of access is by a dangerous vertical ladder.

Top left and right.

The ladder is sturdy, but because its is nearly vertical to the ground, it is not safe for small children.

Bottom left.

A unique feature of this house is a work bench, built directly under the house. It was used for tools and as a sawhorse during the construction.

The platform sills are extended beyond the tree and are butt-joined . The sills are then nailed to the trunk with spike nails.

The tree trunk is not actually inside the house, even though it looks that way in this photo.

View of an inside corner, showing how the corner upright and top wall plates meet in a plain butt joint.

The covering for the roof, walls, and window was scrap plywood sections. Excellent use was made of scrap materials throughout.